Meditations of a Flawed ashlar

BILL HOSLER, PM

Published by Upon The Square Publishing

www.uponthesquare.com

Edited by Philippa Lee

Cover by Al Mahmud

First Edition

ISBN: 978-1544033846

Printed in USA

DEDICATION

To Tammi, my love, my muse, my cheerleader, and my soulmate. Thank you for believing in me and giving me the confidence to reach for the stars

CONTENTS

Acknowledgments

There are so many people I would like to thank: Robert Johnson for encouraging me to start writing, Todd E. Creason for giving me a venue, and the rest of the Midnight Freemasons for helping me learn my craft.

Chris Hodapp, Jeff Naylor, Nate Brindle, and the rest of my colleagues in the Knights of the North for giving me a sound foundation in which to build my Masonic edifice upon.

I would also like to thank Philippa Lee for editing this book, and Brother Adam Thayer for using his grammar Nazi skills for good, hence making me look good!

Especial thanks to Brother Andy Fracica and Worshipful Master Turner England of Highland Lodge #762 for going out of their way to make a special trip to take photographs of the Corinthian of the Fort Wayne Masonic Temple for the cover of this book.

Finally, I want to thank Brother Lance Kates for being a good friend and one of my greatest cheerleaders – I hope he is looking down from the Celestial Lodge Above with approval.

1. Great Masons

A few days ago, I was driving through a neighboring town to run some errands. As I passed by the Masonic temple a mural on the side of the building caught my eye.

I have seen this image a hundred times on the internet. A composite of famous Freemasons gathered together in a painting. Movie stars, politicians, scientists, and cowboys with one thing in common – during their life they had all been members of the Craft. I smiled as I drove by the building. A warm feeling was inside me because I too was a member of that fraternity of great men.

As I was driving my mind began to wander. The reason that mural existed was to show to the outside world the great men who once were Freemasons and encourage them to ask for a petition. It's a great source of pride for us who are members and a great recruiting tool, but that mural only tells part of the story. There are other "Great Masons" we never discuss.

For every famous Mason on that mural there are several thousand unsung great Masons who serve this fraternity every day without thoughts of honors or pay of any kind.

Brother John Smith comes into the temple twice a week to clean the building. For several hours John sweeps floors, cleans the restrooms, restocks the supplies, and makes sure everything is spotless so when the members arrive the place looks and smells good. Brother Smith does such a good job no one ever thinks it ever gets dirty.
Worshipful Brother Marty Jones. Marty works with the new members helping them learn their work. Marty is very patient with the newly obligated Brothers, listening to them repeat the same phrases over and over, helping the newly obligated brother with the pronunciation of these new words to their vocabularies. Most of all giving them encouragement and answering the questions they might have.

Brother Gordon Brown. Brother Brown retired from his job a few years ago and felt something lacking in his life. Gordon began volunteering at the local Veterans' hospital though the Masonic Service Association helping recuperating veterans write letters, talking to them and providing comfort for those who served their country.

There are hundreds of examples of these unsung "Great Masons" throughout the world. Each one doing the small things that combined, like the stones of Solomon's temple, build Freemasonry into a beautiful edifice which unites us into that band of Brothers without the thought of thanks or honors. These men are the true "Masonic secrets".

Originally published on the *Midnight Freemasons* website – August 2013

2. Titles and fancy aprons

When I became a Freemason a little over a decade ago, the number of men knocking on the door of the temple were few. Members of the lodge would get excited when the Secretary mentioned the lodge had a petition. Brothers would scurry to find someone who could play a certain part in the degree work, and everyone started boning up on ritual they hadn't studied in a long time.

Becoming an officer of the lodge during those days was usually easy. If you showed up to lodge you became an officer. When I was raised, I hadn't even considered becoming a lodge officer but the very first meeting I attended as a Master Mason, I sat in as Junior Steward. "Just sit in the chair and do what the Senior Steward does", I was told. "Just stand up and pick up the rod. Don't worry, there aren't any speaking parts." I kept showing up month after month and by default I was the Junior Steward.

As the years progressed so did my offices, until the fateful day I was installed into the Oriental Chair as the Worshipful Master of my lodge, just a little over four years as a Master Mason. When I am asked about my time as Master of my lodge, I usually quote Abraham Lincoln. Lincoln was once asked how he liked being president and Lincoln responded: "You have heard about the man tarred and feathered and ridden out of town on a rail? A man in the crowd asked him how he liked it, and his reply was, 'If it wasn't for the honor of the thing, I would rather walk'."
I
t amazes me how much, in just a few short years of being a Freemason, membership has swelled. When I was going through the degrees I was told by a Brother, "I don't know why you are joining, Masonry is going to be dead in a few years", and now there are lodges that have nearly constant degree work. Mostly I'd suspect this to be because of Dan Brown's books. While this has been great for the fraternity the increase in membership has caused issues few would have thought of just a couple years ago.

Recently I had heard about a young Brother who was expecting to become a lodge officer during the next upcoming Masonic year. When the Senior Warden announced his list of appointed officers for his year, this young Brother's name wasn't on the list. After lodge was closed this Brother became very angry claiming his office was "stolen from him". It was "his turn" and that he had been "cheated". Since then, the young Brother has not come back to the lodge.

I feel for him; in many lodges these days, being a Masonic lodge officer is like trying out for the football team. If you have a lodge where forty men regularly attend and there are only eleven officer positions, someone's not going to make the cut. It's easy math.

I cannot consider what is in the Brother's heart as to why he became so upset that night. It could be that he really did feel it was "his turn", and that he was missing out on some current or future Masonic honor, or it could be that being an officer was the only way he knew that he could serve the Craft.

For the last few decades being an officer and getting an honorary title and a fancy apron was the way you were rewarded for years of dedicated service. It was like one of those punch cards you get when you visit a restaurant, and after each visit an employee punches your card, then after so many visits you get free food. You went through a line in a lodge or appendant body and once you served your time as the head of that group you were given a fancy new apron and a new title, which forevermore will be attached to your name in Masonic circles.

You may think it's easy for me to say these things, since I already had a "PM" behind my name, and this is just a case of "he got his, so he isn't worried about it anymore". But I can assure you this isn't the case.

This young man's response to the slight made me do some deep soul searching. We are told Freemasonry's job is to "make good men better". Serving as an officer of a body might be, and is, a great honor but it isn't going to make you a better man. All of us, regardless of our fancy titles and the color of our aprons must begin to restart the practice of working together, back in the quarries. We must remember there are other ways of serving Freemasonry.

Masonic Charity

Masonic charity is one of the purest forms of our gentle Craft. Extending your hand to help up a Brother who has been knocked down by life; making sure a Brother's widow has enough to eat or her house is warm and in good repair and that the Brother's orphans have clean clothes. Sadly, today many Brothers think that our charity is helping a local school, donating blood, or giving money to some large charity designed to get Masonry good press in the hope that new members will come. These are all worthy charities, but they are not Masonic charity.

Masonic Education

Taking the time to educate yourself might not seem like it is helping Masonry, but it is. The more educated in Masonic knowledge you become, the more you can help share your light with others. As it says in the Charge of an Entered Apprentice: "At your leisure hours, that you may improve in Masonic knowledge, you are to converse with well-informed brethren, who will be always as ready to give, as you will be to receive information."

Serve on a Committee
Every lodge needs things done. Putting together a degree team or repainting the lodge room are just some examples of ways you can be of service. If your lodge building is in perfect condition (and for some reason I doubt that this is the case) you can serve on an investigation committee. There are countless things a man can do to serve his brethren. In a way, it's like starting a business. Find a hole and fill it!

Appendant or Concordant Bodies
First, I am not saying neglect your home lodge by becoming active in another Masonic body. Symbolic lodge should always be your priority but there are many Masonic bodies and most (if not all of them) are starving for membership. Working on a Scottish Rite stage crew or joining a Knights Templar drill team could be fun and you might learn some new skills. It also allows you to work with more charities if that is your thing.

Other Lodges
If you are blessed to belong to a lodge that is healthy and has a thriving membership you may consider finding a lodge that needs help and become a plural member. Maybe your attendance and involvement in the other lodge could help keep it going and maybe it will begin to thrive. I would suggest that if you make this choice, check out the lodge before you join. Sometimes there is a reason a lodge is smaller, and it isn't thriving. Make sure the lodge is a good fit for you.
No matter which option you choose just don't give up. If your goal is to be an officer of a Masonic lodge, one day you will get there. Remember Masonry is a lifetime commitment. Keep working in the quarries until you achieve your goal. Experience will make a better officer when you finally get there, and Freemasonry will make you a better man.

Originally published on the *Midnight Freemasons* website – *November 2015.*

3. Have you made your Mark?

Any Mason who has advanced through the degrees of the York Rite knows the meaning of "making your Mark". For those companions and Sir Knights it means they have added their "Mark" to a book, symbolically linking them to the cathedral builders of ancient times. Most of you created your Mark and handed it to the recorder of the group and went on with life and the other degrees.

In the world of the profane, most people believe the phrase "making your mark" means you have created a long-lasting impression on someone, or the world itself. You have added something positive that will be remembered after you passed to the Celestial Lodge above. It's another Masonic phrase that has become a household phrase, even though the original meaning has faded away.

One question I ask myself is "have I made a mark on my lodge?" Years from now, once I leave this planet will the members of my lodge remember me or any of my works? Will something I have done or said be referenced years from now? Many will say, "Of course I will be remembered. My picture is on the wall of the lodge with the other Past Masters!" But is your photograph, along with one hundred other men leaving your mark? How many times have you looked at one of these photos and truly known anything about the man in the photo? Usually, I just look at them and think how much the clothing styles have changed since the year the photo was taken. In my opinion, the photo is a memorial, not a lasting impression.

Some would say the best way to leave your mark would be in your active participation in lodge. Being a long-time lodge secretary or being the chairman of a committee for several decades would leave a lasting impression. These are great ways to serve your lodge. But make no mistake, after several years the memory of your participation will wither away.

In my humble opinion, the best way to leave your mark on the lodge is the way in which you interact with your brethren and teach them to become better men and Masons. Whether you realize it or not, the other Brethren look at you, especially the younger men and hold you up to be an example of how they should conduct themselves in life as well as inside a tiled lodge room. These men want and need guidance on their journey through the Craft.

They begin judging us from the moment they walk through the front door of our temple. If they walk in the door and see a building in disrepair, dingy walls, broken furniture and get hit in the face with that familiar "old person smell" – like they are walking into their grandparent's house – that will leave a lasting impression, but sadly not a good one.

These young men are looking for positive men, and a positive atmosphere, which will help them become better men. When they see you sitting on the sidelines chatting while the lodge is conducting candidates during degree work, falling asleep, or the lodge having the same argument every month during a stated meeting, it won't take them long to realize we don't have the answers they are looking for; or even worse, we aren't providing what we tell these men we give them when they ask for a petition. Remember Brethren, these men are the ones who are checking to see how square your ashlar truly is.

It has now been many years since that warm night in June when I first knocked on the door of my lodge and asked to be made a Mason. But I will never forget the brethren assembled who befriended me and taught me how to be a just and upright Mason and a better man. Sadly, many of these Brothers are no longer with us, but I think about them each and every day. Their memories bring a smile to my face. Each one of these men "made their mark" on my soul and created lifelong memories for me. Many of the things these brethren taught me, I try to convey to you in my writings.

I hope some of my words inspire you to be a better man and Freemason and help me "make my mark" upon your living stone and in turn, help me honor these men.

4. The fraternity needs a lighthouse

Recently I saw a photo of a lighthouse being hit with a giant tidal wave. Mother Nature hit this edifice with everything she had, and it not only withstood the force of the wave, but the lighthouse continued to stand and its beacon still shining light to the world.

Lighthouses are designed to warn ships of upcoming dangers, coral reefs, shoals, shallow water, and harbor entrances; anything that may cause a vessel to sink, incur damage or cause loss of life. Their light shines to make navigating the seas a better, safer place.
When constructing a lighthouse, the builder would pick a level area on which to lay a solid foundation using only the finest materials available to him in. Upon the foundation, the more modern lighthouses were built using rocks or stones cemented together into one majestic edifice which, if properly maintained, can withstand the elements, and continue to be at the benefit of man for an eternity.

I would like to think our gentle Craft is much like that lighthouse. Our fraternity was built upon a solid foundation of faith, hope and charity. Each stone of that lighthouse is emblematic of the brethren, which comprise the membership of our Craft. Each one of us were once rough stones which, much like the Temple of King Solomon, were chiseled and shaped by the builder with the working tools of Masonry until those stones, like us, were hewed, squared and leveled to the builder's requirements.

These stones are united into one common mass and strengthened by the spreading of cement which, when hardened, allowed the builder to complete this collection of individual stones into a structure which produces light, and which when used properly can help us ward off all approaching danger and become a benefit to mankind for the ages to come.

The world will never know how many people throughout history were saved from an early, watery grave because the light from those lighthouses alerted the crews of those vessels and kept them on a safe path to their destination. Much like we will never know how many men have been saved from a life of disrepute and dishonor because they were taught and learned to apply the teachings of our humble Craft to their life and used the light of Freemasonry to help them subdue their passions.

Any man-made structure requires constant maintenance to ensure its long-time service. Preservationists must continue to inspect and repair parts of the building which have begun to weaken or fall apart. The light source, which is the reason for the building's existence, must also be constantly maintained or the source replaced and perhaps upgraded to ensure the lighthouse's relevance. If the lighthouse no longer produces light, chances are the edifice would be abandoned and the entire building would begin to crumble and eventually, cease to exist.

Many people contend Freemasonry has begun to follow down the path of that neglected lighthouse. In our zeal for greatness in numbers, we have ceased to continue to maintain or upgrade our light source.

Dues which no longer cover the costs of running our lodges and the living stones have begun to crumble away. The cement which should merge us into one sacred band of friends and Brothers has begun to crack as our meetings which were once a source of enlightenment and friendship have degraded into a two-hour long argument over the costs of basic supplies like toilet paper and light bulbs. Like pieces of dried mortar our members drop away never to be seen again.

Even when the brethren want to maintain their symbolic lighthouse, often they aren't allowed to even try because of the "building codes" of a faraway Grand Lodge who micromanage and oversee everything. Many common and sensible solutions cannot be applied to fix their lighthouse because of the over regulations of Grand lodges and when the workers asked the reason for the rule, they are told it's because "we've always done it that way". All the while, the stones begin to fall away from our lighthouse and sadly can't be replaced. These poor workmen must stand by and watch in frustration as their beloved structure falls apart.

The light source itself may also become dim from lack of maintenance. A century ago, the light was produced by a single source, provided by a candle or a lamp which was reflected into a large lens and then it was magnified, and could be seen for miles. Think about that: one spark from a small candle or lamp could provide lifesaving light for miles away. What if the fuel source for that light wasn't replenished on a regular basis? Without the fuel, there is no light, and the entire shore would be cast into darkness; vessels approaching the perils of the shore would not receive warning and their passengers would perish.

Sadly, in the last half century our lodges have not been replacing the fuel of Masonic light, allowing many of the followers of King Solomon to be cast into the darkness. Lodge meetings have become a place to discuss fundraisers to supplement the deficit in the lodge treasury, with unrealistically low dues and charity events which will get the lodge's name in the local newspaper in hopes of bringing more men to the door of the lodge. The source of light being Masonic education and charity have been extinguished in an attempt to bring in new members.

The light of Masonry has been dimmed in our lodges because in the last half century our fraternity has chosen bureaucracy and membership numbers over Masonic education and Masonic charity.

When the light of a lighthouse has been dimmed due to circumstances like fog, the keeper will turn on a foghorn. A foghorn is a device which emits a loud sound to warn vessels when the lighthouse is too dim to be seen; a loud cry in the darkness to warn others in order that they may ward off all approaching danger.

I hope this chapter will act as a foghorn, which warns others of the dangers of a dimmed light source. The Grand Edifice of Freemasonry may be in a state of disrepair, but it is far from being at the point it needs to be torn down. Our foundation is as solid and level as it was when it was first laid.

We must begin to repair what time and neglect have done to our lighthouse using quality materials and upgrade all operation systems to ensure we can withstand whatever is being thrown at us and to keep our light shining for centuries to come.

Originally published on the *Midnight Freemasons* website – *February 2016*

5. To learn to subdue my passions

To learn to subdue my passions. As Freemasons, we have heard this phrase many times. Chances are you have even recited it. Have you truly thought about it what it means?

To be completely honest, when I asked a friend of mine for a petition to join the Craft, I really had no idea what Masonry was about or what it offered. I had never heard the slogan – "We make good men better" – I just remember some friends of my parents who would come to the house when I was a small child, and several of them wore a Masonic ring.

Many times, since becoming a Master Mason, I've asked myself "How does attending lodge make me a better man?" It can't be the meal we serve or the opening of the lodge, it sure isn't the Secretary reading last month's minutes or Brother Treasurer telling the members how much money we have in the bank account. I was beginning to think I was missing the point.

It finally occurred to me one night, while sitting in the lodge room as the lodge officers were opening the lodge. Whilst my premise may be simplistic, I feel it is fairly accurate. I also believe all Masons feel these things are important, but I think the different generations place the importance in different areas for different reasons.

To learn: You have been learning since your mother gave birth to you. You learned to sit up, talk, and eat without assistance before your first birthday. As you progressed in age you attended school. You never quit learning. The question remains, what can you learn from attending lodge?

As you progress through your degrees you hear certain words and phrases. At first these words sound unusual because they are phrased in a way in which our language is no longer spoken. Understanding what is being said to you is difficult at first to understand because you aren't used to being spoken to in such an old tongue. I believe this is why the Craft asks you to memorize the work. Repetition and memorization help your brain convert these words from gibberish to a beautifully spoken and largely forgotten language.

Sadly, today in Masonry we are convinced that the only reason we memorize these works is so we can advance to the next degree or learn the remaining ritual so we can help with the performing of the degree work. I truly believe this is one of the reasons men find it so hard to discover what they are looking for in our fraternity.

In my opinion memorization for advancement is only a small part of the catechism or lesson to be learned. Whether we realize it or not our ritual isn't just a bunch of words thrown together to sound pretty and impress people. The ritual is a roadmap for our journey to the East to find that which was lost.

Each word of that beautifully phrased script is designed to be studied. I feel the archaic language is designed not to just sound impressive but to pique your curiosity and encourage you to research what you've heard. Each word and syllable should be dissected and studied to find out its meaning.

Floor work is also very instructive. If you have taken an office in your lodge or filled a chair for an absent officer, I know you have encountered the floor work. When I was a young officer, I hated floor work. No matter how hard I tried after we closed, I had a Past Master approach me to tell me how I was doing the floor work wrong. Sometimes, I would have several of them approach me at the same time to explain my errors and would get into a big argument about how I screwed it up. They would stand there and bicker back and forth about my transgressions and I would walk away, and they never even noticed I left!

These Brethren who were trying to help me have been told since they were new in the Craft how important the proper execution of the floor work is and wanted to stress the importance of it to me. Proper floor work is important for several reasons. First it does impress the candidate and secondly, when properly done, is very beautiful to watch. These Brethren, while well-meaning, in my opinion missed the importance of this essential lodge function.

Whether it is within the opening or closing of a lodge or within degree work, the floor work was designed to teach our brethren about symbolism. Each step you take or how the deacons and stewards hold their rods is designed to display symbols in which, when researched give you a nugget of information in which you can add to your knowledge and ultimately to your self-improvement. Sadly, most of these subtle movements are lost on the brethren who it is meant to instruct.

Expanding your mind through the study behind the ritual and understanding the symbolism which is hidden within the floor work of the lodge is the first upright step on your journey from the darkness toward the light of self-improvement.

To subdue my passions: The second upright step in your journey to become a better man is learning to subdue your passions. I feel this phrase means learning to do things in moderation. We all know the Junior Warden is supposed to watch over the Craft assembled and ensure that no one converts "refreshment into excess" or doesn't have too much of a good thing. This is a lesson that is important to everyone. I also feel we must each subdue our passions for different things. For some people their passion is alcohol, for others it is relationships, or tobacco. You can become addicted to many things. My passion was with food.

When I was raised to the sublime degree of a Master Mason, I weighed nearly 500 pounds. I lived a sedentary lifestyle and the darkness made me feel truly miserable and helpless. As I came to light, I started to study and read every Masonic book I could find and truly began to embrace the fraternity, I realized that if I would simply "try to subdue my passion" and just eat half of what I would normally eat at a meal, I would take in half the calories. I started calling this my "Masonic diet". Eventually, I began to lose weight and I am now down to a more manageable size.

Each of us has passions we find difficulty in subduing. In my opinion, the self-reflection we learn through the study of Masonry and its symbols will help you identify the passion, to place you on the right path to gaining control. I'm not saying it will be easy but since your faith is in God and is well founded with prayer and self-control, you will be successful.

Improve myself in Masonry: Each of these upright steps will help us improve ourselves in Masonry. Self-improvement, like Masonry is a lifelong journey, one we will never complete. I feel the third upright step is continuing your journey by attending your lodge.

Each of us, no matter who we are, need help in maintaining the progress we have made through learning and in the fight to subdue our passions. Interacting with Brethren who are on the same journey of improvement as you are, should give you motivation to continue your work and help encourage another brother to work harder on his goals. Spreading the cement of Brotherly love does strengthen each of us.

I know it is hard to see how sitting through a long dreary meeting of minutes and paying bills will make you a better man, but if you can look past what Masonry has become and try to see "what has been lost", maybe you can find the working tools in the ritual to help transform your rough ashlar into something that's a bit more perfect

Originally published on the *Midnight Freemasons* website – *April 2016*

6. Burnouts and buffets

I just finished reading a piece written by fellow Midnight Freemason contributor, my friend, and Brother Robert Johnson, called "Is the honeymoon over?" As I sat here reading his work, I noticed myself nodding my head in agreement with every word RJ had written.

I have a rather unique position in the Craft; I am not an old Mason, but I am not a new guy either. At the time of writing this piece, I became an Entered Apprentice fourteen years ago. From the time I signed my petition, I couldn't wait until I was a Master Mason. Before the ink was dry on my signature, I was looking at Masonic books and Masonic rings. I couldn't believe how slow the petition process was, and the thought of waiting between degrees was agony!

The night I was raised, I couldn't believe I had finally made it. I was a fully-fledged, bona-fide Freemason; I began to feel like a dog who caught the car – "I caught it, now what do I do with it?" Luckily, my question was answered before I exited the lodge room.

For nearly each hand I shook in congratulations, another hand contained a petition for another Masonic body. From the Shriners to the Scottish Rite and the York Rite; I had an application for all of them. I placed them in my pocket and went home, my mind was on overload with all I had seen and had done that night.

Within the next three months I had become a member of everything: the Shriners, the Scottish Rite, and the York Rite, along with such groups as the Philalethes Society. My wallet began to explode with dues cards!

Once the dues cards were in place, the offices came. At my first lodge meeting as a Master Mason I became Junior Steward, and since I had shown the brethren, I had an ability to memorize, I also received multiple pieces of ritual to learn. I was asked if I wouldn't mind filling a chair in one of the York Rite bodies. In my zeal I agreed, and I received an office in the body of the local York Rite, and with the jewels of the office came even more ritual to memorize.

I can honestly say I gave Masonry my all. I had a meeting nearly every night for almost seven years. I became a Past Master and a Past High Priest in my Royal Arch Chapter. Along the path I picked up other responsibilities. I was a member of a Grand Lodge committee, and I became a webmaster for a Grand York Rite. I gathered even more jobs within my local Shrine temple, and I can honestly say I mostly loved every minute of it.

However, with problems within my family and my job, the burnout set in. Real life began to invade my Masonic fantasy. The 24-inch gauge I had thrown away came back with a vengeance. The politics I once shrugged off began to anger me. The pieces of ritual I had been juggling for four different Masonic bodies no longer came easy to me. The representation of King Solomon's Temple I built within myself fell apart and I went into a Masonic funk. I guess it could be called a period of Masonic darkness.

Just as Brother RJ wrote, Masonic burnout set in. For the longest time, I was like everyone else, I thought burnout was a bad thing. But much like a forest fire removes the rubbish and allows new life to set in, maybe Masonic burnout can be useful as well. If you go to a drag race, people talk about burnouts as an exciting and positive thing. A burnout is when you make your rear wheels spin as fast as you can while sitting in place with your foot on the brake. When a drag racer brings his car to the racetrack, in his preparation to race he will intentionally burn out his tires, which gets them warm and helps create traction which, if properly done can be the difference between winning or losing the race.

As I'm sure you have been told many times "Masonry is a marathon, not a sprint". That is all well and true, but if you don't get warmed up and gain traction, you will fail at that race. Why not try a little of everything and find out what parts of Masonry you like and discover the ones that aren't for you? Much like an all-you-can-eat buffet: on the first trip most people mound their plates with as many types of food as they can heap on. When they return to the buffet a second time, they have a better idea of what dishes they want to eat and only fill their plate with the ones they liked.

After a period of Masonic inactivity and self-reflection, I got my life back on track and began to think about the parts of Freemasonry I liked and missed, and the parts I could live without. I realized that being approached with the possibilities of Grand Offices, and the honors I received, gave me a swelled head and I lost my perspective. I began to look at the fraternity in a different way. I also discovered, thanks to Brother Johnson, that I enjoyed writing about Masonic topics. My burnout period also provided experiences for writing. It allowed me to use the experiences as "teachable moments".

Don't get me wrong: I'm not advocating that you take your zeal for Freemasonry and fill every night with a different meeting. I advocate moderation, not excess. Use your experience to find your place within your fraternity. If you find your place, you are more likely to get the traction you will need to make that sprint into a marathon.

If you only take one thing away from this piece, it's DON'T QUIT! You joined this fraternity for a reason. Don't stop searching until you find it. Don't let the bickering or the politics, or even some of the rules you find silly, discourage you and make you demit. These silly things will eventually go away. Masonry is just like life. There will be things you love and things you hate. Just take it all in your stride and make the fraternity yours.

Originally published on the *Midnight Freemasons* website – *July 2016*

7. Cereal box Freemasonry

When I was a kid, I would get up early to watch the cartoons on television. Between cartoons, I would watch the commercials the network would play. There were commercials for dolls and action figures, various other toys, but the commercials I remember most were the advertisements selling breakfast cereals. These commercials could span from Tony the Tiger telling me that I should want Frosted Flakes, to Bruce Jenner telling me how Wheaties made it possible for him to win the gold at the Olympics (yes, I'm that old). Each one of these commercials had a few things in common: 1. the product in the commercial tasted awesome, and 2. each one of these boxes of cereal had a prize laying at the bottom.

The prizes they showed looked amazing. I could picture myself having a great time playing with the toys, just like the kids in the commercial I was watching. I would fantasize about the fun I would have if I could convince my mother I needed, and would eat, this cereal. This was not an easy task. My father worked hard but Mom only had a limited amount she could spend on groceries, she tried to stretch every penny.

If I was lucky enough, I could convince my mom that I really liked this product, and she would pick it up for me at the grocery store. When I got home, I would rip open the box and dump the entire contents of the box into a mixing bowl until I heard the clink of the prize falling into the bowl. Giddy with excitement I ran outside to play with this amazing new toy (after trying to fit all that cereal back into the box and set it in the cupboard stuffed with the other opened boxes of cereal I hadn't eaten yet). Once I began to play with the toy, I realized the toy in the bottom of the box that I begged my mom to buy was a plastic piece of junk. The prize in the box was nothing like the toy I had seen on the television commercial; it was either flimsy and broke right away, or it just didn't work. I felt cheated, and the only people that made out well were the owners of the cereal company.

Every year, Masonic membership numbers continue to shrink. Grand Lodges continue to wring their hands and try to come up with new ways to package the fraternity like a product, and pique men's curiosity enough to entice them to join to swell our ranks. A Grand Lodge or appendant body will approach an advertising agency, and television commercials are created; these days, even a social media campaign is created.

These commercials offer friendship, networking which promises to help advance your career, a chance to "Make a Difference" and fulfill a need to give back to the community by participating in charity (or whatever the advertising agencies polling unit tells them what young men of a certain age group want). The agency then puts together a presentation to the Masonic body, and if the Grand Lodge Officers like what they see, they purchase ad time which is targeted to a certain age group of young men. Freemasonry then crosses its fingers and waits for the young men to come to and ask for a petition.

After seeing the commercial, the young man gets excited. Maybe this group sounds like just the thing he has been looking for to complete his life, or he remembers Freemasonry from a Dan Brown movie he watched. He visits an open house at a Masonic Temple near him. Looking around this magnificent building from another era, he gets excited and fills out a petition. His Masonic career slowly starts to go forward, and he cannot wait until he is told to report for his degree work.

After receiving a summons from his lodge to begin his Masonic journey, he begins the degree work. For several months, the young brother spends his free time memorizing the proficiency he is told he needs to know to finally advance toward the goal he is seeking: to be a Master Mason, to learn all the secrets he has been promised and start the journey of self-enlightenment that the commercials and his new brethren have promised him. Finally, that magical day arrives, and he has been raised. He can now sit in lodge, join other Masonic groups, and finally wear that Masonic ring he had already purchased.

Now it's meeting night. The first stated meeting he can attend and participate in because he is now a full-fledged Mason. The newly obligated Brother slowly puts on his best suit, making sure his tie is straight. He admires himself in the mirror thinking how he looks like a Freemason already. The excitement continues to build inside him. He gets to the lodge early so he can get a seat right up front. "I want to be able to get a good view of everything", he thinks to himself. Meeting time comes and the room isn't even half full. On counting he realizes there are only seven other Masons in the audience, "Must be a slow night," he tells himself.

This brother sits on the edge of his seat waiting to be blown away with all the secrets he was promised. He sits through the half hour of the Secretary reading minutes of last month's meeting, and the minutes from all the called meetings for his degree work. He chuckles to himself because he was there for all of that, he really didn't need to hear about it again.

Once the minutes are read, he listens to motions be made to give money to several Masonic youth groups for their Grand sessions. He votes to give them the money, to seem like he knows what is going on, even though he has no clue what he is voting for. The manager of the temple stands before the group and informs the brethren present that the old lawn mower the temple has owned for forty years is broken again and the mechanic states it can no longer be repaired. A new mower needs to be purchased. Several men stand up to argue about the cost of buying a new lawn mower for their temple; the argument seems to last forever. Finally, a committee is formed to approach a member of the lodge who never attends but owns a hardware store to see if he will provide a new mower free of charge or at a deep discount. Then the meeting ends, and everyone dashes out of the building like it's on fire.

The young man just sits there in his seat, dumbfounded. He still doesn't understand how this is going to make him a better man – "Maybe it was just an off night", he decides. After attending for several months, he becomes disillusioned with his lodge and with Freemasonry, and he ceases to attend. At the end of the year, he ignores the dues notices which the lodge sends him and allows his membership to be suspended for nonpayment. Sadly, nobody even noticed he wasn't there.

Just like the child who expects the toy at the bottom of the cereal box to be the greatest thing in his young life, he becomes disillusioned with this new toy and casts it aside as something cheap and not worthy of his time, just a piece of junk. Like the owner of the cereal company, the only one who benefits is the Grand Lodge who received his fees.

Brethren, those of us who decided to continue to pursue Freemasonry knows what this young man received wasn't junk. Freemasonry, when practiced correctly, is a beautiful and life changing experience. We have learned to "package" our fraternity to entice new members to join; what we need to learn now is what is called "service after the sale". Masonically, we can call it providing Brotherly love, relief and truth.

Brotherly love: Instead of just promising to be a positive force in a man's life, let's be that positive force! Instead of an evening of minutes, treasurer's reports and bickering, maybe we can provide the feeling of Brotherhood and education. Make sure to include this new Brother in upcoming lodge events, invite him and his family to dinner or a cookout. Or even a "Brothers-only night" for a drink and conversation. Even something as simple as inviting him to eat at your table in the lodge dining hall. Positive social interaction with a new member will make him feel wanted, and he will want to become a valuable lodge member.

Relief: Remember that part of the obligation that says, "I will help, aid and assist all poor and distressed Master Masons, their widows and orphans"? Maybe we should try doing that! Instead of sending a sympathetic card to a brother who we have heard is sick and offer to pray for him at the next meeting, get several Brothers together and visit him. Take a bag of groceries with you. If he needs help getting to a doctor's appointment, give him a ride. Be there for a Brother who is laying on that darkened square and offer to take his hand and raise him to his feet.

Truth: When young men are asked why they joined Masonry, most will answer "Masonic education". We tell them their pursuit is truly laudable, but we never fulfill their request. Sadly, education is one of the most basic, easiest requests we can fulfill. Many lodges don't want to prolong the length of a stated meeting with education (or suffer the wagging finger of the Past Masters who want to vote on business then go home), so education is dropped to the wayside. Or worse yet, a Brother will stand up and read a piece he printed from the Internet about the Masonic membership of George Washington. With little substance, the "education box" can now be checked off on a Grand Lodge form so that the lodge can apply for a special award.

To receive the maximum benefit of education, pick a non-meeting night and have a group of Brethren gather to have an "education" night. This could be a group who decides to have a book club (yes, like Oprah) where a mutually chosen book is discussed. The discussion can be as deep or as shallow as the group wishes. Another idea would be for the brethren to take turns writing research papers and discussing them in the group. The possibilities are endless!

I would even suggest education need not be limited to Masonic subjects. Invite a tailor to discuss the benefit of owning a custom suit, or an expert on manners. Young men have a lot of questions, and sometimes they have difficulty finding answers to their questions. Be their source of light which will help them become a better man. The best part is that informal education nights can be conducted anywhere, including locations where you can enjoy fellowship over a drink.

Brethren, these are just a few ideas in which we can provide "service after the sale". I'm sure you and the members of your lodge can come up with dozens more. Not only will Masonry not be a cheap prize at the bottom of a cereal box, but we will elevate it to the ultimate treasure that keeps on giving.

Originally published on the *Midnight Freemasons* website – *September 2016*

8. As the sun is in the south

"As the sun is in the south is at meridian height it is the glory and beauty of the day".
I know most of you have heard a phrase like this while you have attended lodge (your actual ritual may vary). The sun is at its highest point in the sky and the rays of light cast down on us, illuminating the great works of the Supreme Architect of the Universe. During this point of the day most of us follow the lead of the Junior Warden and take time to rest and refresh ourselves before returning to our labors.

Since most of us labor at our vocations during the daylight, we never stop and consider that some men work at various times around the clock. Much like the twenty-four-inch gauge, the workday is divided into three equal parts: day shift, or as most of us refer to it as "first shift", the evening shift or second shift, and the night shift, which is commonly known as third shift (or by its nickname "the graveyard shift"). Some jobs are scheduled differently than above but, as a hard and fast rule, most workers generally fall into one of these eight-hour shifts.

At the time when you are about to cease your labors and go home, many men are rising and on their way to their jobs in the evening, and still others are about to go home when you arrive in the morning at your workplace. Today's world requires people to be working at various hours around the clock.

Rarely are these men thought of when we think about Freemasonry. I know that many men, at one point myself included, have had to reluctantly quit attending their lodge's regularly stated meetings and degree work because their regular vocation forced them to work in the evenings. It's sad because they then miss the fellowship which being a Mason brings. They must abandon their Masonic career to pursue their vocational career.

Many times, I have seen a young man join our fraternity and be rushed through degrees in a one-day class or on a Saturday morning. Once he is raised, you don't see him again, not because he is disgruntled with the fraternity but because he works a different shift. He becomes just a card-carrying member through no fault of his own because he has to provide for his family. In a way, it could be said that everyone benefits in this situation. The lodge gets his yearly dues and the Brother gets to claim the title of Freemason.

This arrangement has worked for decades. While we are told our families and our usual vocations aren't to take a backseat to our gentle Craft, a Brother who doesn't have the opportunity to attend lodge regularly does miss out on the fellowship of his Brother Masons and, at times, good and wholesome instruction, which could possibly make him into the better man he professed he wished to become.

We as a fraternity are also missing many opportunities not only to increase our membership, but to better use the resources we already possess. I believe we should encourage the creation of more daylight lodges within our jurisdictions. Daylight lodges are simply lodges that meet during the daytime instead of the evening; everything else is the same except the time of day!

Almost every Masonic temple in North America (or around the world for that matter) sits idle for twenty hours a day, six days a week, unless there are multiple bodies meeting within the building during the month, but even then, the edifice is empty and idle for the majority of the time. The building is still being heated and cooled, but no one is using the building. To me that seems like a waste of resources. Especially when we have so many current and potential Brethren who could be using the building.

If a daylight lodge is chartered within the temple, not only will it put this space to better use, but there is potential that Masonry in your area may receive new members it wouldn't receive in lodges that only meet at traditional times; such as younger men with different work schedules, men with young children who wish to stay home with their family at night, or even retirees who can no longer attend lodge at night because their eyesight has gotten to the point they can no longer drive in the dark.

Many of these retirees could also benefit these new lodges; most of these men are long time members, even possibly Past Masters who can help direct the newer members in building their lodge. It also gives retirees a reason to get out of the house and socialize. A lodge could be opened at ten or eleven a.m. and once business or degree work has ceased and lodge closes, they could serve a lunch at noon, just in time for members on second shift to make their way to their jobs.

Another benefit could be that brethren of other lodges who work during the day could take their lunch breaks at the temple and "spread cement" before going back to work! Nothing could be better for Freemasonry than for Brethren gathering for a few moments between their individual labors.

I have heard concerns from some Brothers that a lodge which is open during the day may become a place where men gather for networking and socializing instead of for the lodges intended purpose. I believe it could happen; I have known lodges that meet in the evening that become the same thing.

Each individual lodge is like an individual person, they have their own personality and are conducted by the will of its members. I believe if the numbers allow it that several daylight lodges could be chartered, and a potential member should visit several lodges before he asks for a petition, much like he would at a conventional nighttime lodge, to find the right fit for him. If several exist, he has a better chance in which suits his needs.

If one or more chartered daylight lodges are successful in your community, other appendant and concordant bodies may also form new bodies: like a daytime York Rite body, Shrine club, or even a Scottish Rite club. How wonderful would it be to have many healthy, active Masonic bodies meeting in your building? Not only will it make Masonry stronger but think of the extra revenue more dues will bring in!

Brethren, Freemasonry can be just as active while the sun is in the south, as it is as when it's in the West at the close of the day. Let us think outside the box and put our members, potential members, and resources to better uses.

Originally published on the *Midnight Freemasons* website – *December 2016*

9. Dangerous travels

Recently, I've been thinking about the founding of my mother Grand Lodge in Indiana. In 2018, the Grand Lodge of Indiana will celebrate their bicentennial. In January 1818, Freemasons from nine lodges, working under charters by the Grand Lodge of Kentucky and the Grand Lodge of Ohio gathered in Madison, Indiana to start the process of organizing their own future.

Back in that day, there were very few choices of transportation by which you could travel across a newly formed state; you could travel by riverboat down the Ohio river (if your town was near the river and you could afford the fare), you could travel via horseback (down rough paths which could hardly qualify as a trail), and if you didn't own a horse, you walked.

No matter which mode of transportation you chose, the journey was guaranteed to be uncomfortable; muddy trails, snow and high winds combined to make the trip difficult. Depending on where you lived, your destination may be several days (or even weeks) away. In the winter you slept on the cold ground, shivering under a blanket near a fire, eating what meager provisions you brought. During the summer, you endured the heat of the day and hordes of insects. You might encounter highwaymen who would think nothing of robbing you of all your possessions and leaving you for dead in the wilderness. You always ran the risk of a wild animal who might see you as a threat to his domain and an easy dinner. There was no 911 or Auto Club to come to your rescue if you were in trouble. You were on your own.

No matter how you traveled, when you arrived at your destination the accommodations were scant at best. Most of these men would stay in the home of another Freemason or in a local inn. Tavern owners usually offered beds above their establishments; you paid to spend the night and you shared that bed with all the other travelers. You ate what the tavern served that day. Once your business was complete, you began your return trip home facing the same dangers and discomforts as before.

These men so believed in the Craft that they were willing to endure all these hardships and dangers, not to mention the days of being away from their families and livelihoods, all in order to help advance the Craft.

Traveling wasn't the only hardships our forefathers had to endure. We are taught that Masons originally met in high hills or low vales, which later became the upstairs loft spaces of inns and taverns, accessible only by climbing a ladder. I have heard stories of lodges meeting in caves, in barns, sometimes even in the home of one of the brothers. One thing is for certain, most of these spaces were not ideal for a lodge meeting. Before a lodge was opened, the Masons had to get to work setting up the room, moving the chairs into position, laying out the jewels and the aprons. If degree work was to happen that night, a brother would draw out the tracing boards on the floor which had to be mopped up after the lodge was closed. Once the lodge was closed, the furniture in the space had to be moved back to its normal position. These buildings were drafty, cold and uncomfortable to occupy.

Over the last century, we Freemasons have become accustomed to meeting in beautiful lodge buildings. Sometimes these edifices were marble palaces in the center of a big city, other times a modest room above a storefront in a small town. These buildings all have modern plumbing, are heated for the winter and sometimes even air conditioned for a pleasant climate in the summertime. Custom furniture was commissioned and purchased which never had to be moved. Beautiful carpets lay on the floor beneath the feet of the brethren.

It's difficult today for us to imagine the travel involved and the meeting places that our forefathers used to spread the light of Masonry. Sometimes just the events surrounding these men's lives added even more issues for these men to bear.

Most of us know that throughout the last few centuries many Grand Lodges issued emergent charters to men in order to meet during war time. The daily lives of these men are the hardest thing for me in my comfortable modern life to fathom.

These men would march for hours a day, usually with little sleep and even less food, to a battlefield where they had to make camp, and then risk their lives on the field of battle. Once the battle was over, if they survived the conflict and weren't too badly injured, the men would erect a tent, get out the trunk of Masonic regalia from a wagon, and open a lodge. Sometimes lodge officers had to be continually re-elected, not because the brother quit the lodge, but because the man had been killed on the field of battle. Think of it: these men were hungry, exhausted, and trying to forget the horrors of war they had witnessed that day, but they still thought enough of their obligation to continue to meet, just like they would have back in their homes.

Throughout history, our Masonic forefathers endured hardships of all kinds just to practice what today we take for granted. From rough travel to bad living and meeting accommodations, to actually risking their lives on battlefields or being tortured in a prison camp for their belief in Freemasonry.

Sadly, not all these hardships are in our past. Many continue to this day. I recently had the distinct honor to speak with a Brother who asked that I keep his name and his home secret, not because he was worried about his own safety (he escaped and is now in a free country) but because the Brethren of his lodge in his home country are still in peril.

This Brother belongs to a lodge in the Middle East. His government has declared Freemasonry illegal. If the location of his lodge is discovered by their local government, his Brothers will be arrested, placed in prison, and after they are tortured into confessing crimes against the state, they would be executed. Despite the risk, they still meet on a regular basis, in a secret lodge room. They meet and discuss Freemasonry and how it helps them in their lives. While meeting, they keep an eye on each other and if a member or his family needs Masonic charity, they will quietly arrange it. They don't allow a dictatorship or the threat of death to stop their belief in the obligation they took.

Brother! After reading this short piece, I want to ask you a question: if these men can attend lodge with zeal and enthusiasm despite all these hardships, why don't you attend lodge? If our forefathers could risk their lives to the elements of weather and rough travel for days to attend a meeting, why can't you get in your well heated and air-conditioned car to drive less than an hour on a well-built road to visit a lodge in a well heated or air-conditioned building with running water and electricity to spend an hour with the brethren of your lodge? If the men in a secret lodge living under a dictatorship can sneak away in the dark of night in secret to meet under the possibility of being tortured and executed, why can't you endure the reading of the minutes or a treasurer's report? Is listening to Past Masters arguing about of the price of light bulbs the reason that keeps you away from a group of men you swore to treat as your Brother help him in his time of need?

No. I didn't think so.

I'm not saying dealing with our troubles are trivial. We all have a lot of current issues within our lodge rooms. But is quitting going to change them? No! The only thing not attending lodge will do is allow the problems to get worse and eventually put our fraternity of the ash heap of history.

Instead of everyone quitting the Craft, why not find kindred spirits within your lodge and start changing what you don't like? Think of it this way: if your lodge only has eight regular attendees, if you and nine other Brethren vote to do something, you will win the majority. If your numbers continue to grow you and your brothers can start to transform the lodge into a place you can look forward to attending, chances are your changes will entice new men into joining your lodge. If for some reason this doesn't work, check with your Grand Lodge and see how many Master Masons it takes to start a new lodge.

Most of the hardships I have listed above, and many others I don't have the space to mention, can be fixed with hard work, perseverance, and time. Roads were built, money was raised for new, comfortable meeting accommodations, and lodges were arranged in secret to protect those in countries where Masonry is still illegal. Whining and quitting has never fixed anything. Neither has letting someone else deal with it. It's time for all of us to stand up, roll up our sleeves and make Freemasonry the fraternity we want it to be and that it should be.

Originally published on the *Midnight Freemasons* website – *February 2017*

10. Living stones or bricks?

"But we, as Free and Accepted Masons, are taught to make use of it for the more noble and glorious purpose of divesting our minds and consciences of all the vices and superfluities of life, thereby fitting ourselves as living stones for that spiritual building, that house not made with hands, eternal in the heavens."

Every Freemason knows the above quote as the speculative use of the common gavel given to an Entered Apprentice. We are told that we are to use the working tools of Freemasonry to try to work on our imperfect ashlars and square them in the hopes of becoming a perfect ashlar to fit the needs of the builder, which in this case is the Supreme Architect of the Universe.

In my entire Masonic career, I've always pictured this perfect ashlar to be completely squared or oblong, like a brick, which would fit easily into a building, spiritual or otherwise. I guess I got this impression from looking at the examples of a perfect and imperfect ashlar sitting on the floor of the East in my mother lodge.

Recently, while listening to a radio program, I heard the host of the show ask a question to his audience "Are we living stones or are we bricks?" The host further explained that stones are made by our creator from different materials which can be collected from all over the world. Each stone differs in size, color, and shape, and have different strengths and weaknesses. Each of these stones is beautiful in its own right.

The host further elaborated that those bricks are artificial. They are made from materials created by men and formed into square bricks. Each of these bricks are identical. Nothing special about them. They are created to make an edifice for strength, not beauty. "If you look at a house of bricks, it isn't going to be as beautiful as a house made of natural field stones", the host stated.

To be completely honest, the host's words shocked me. I began to feel a dilemma build inside myself. Was the host correct? How can a Mason be a living stone, and square himself at the same time? Are these two thoughts polar opposites of each other?

I began to research the topic of ashlars, both perfect and imperfect. According to Mackey's *Encyclopedia of Freemasonry*, Sir Christopher Wren, in a memorandum about the building of St Paul's Cathedral in London, stated that an ashlar "was a stone, ready-dressed from the quarries for use in walls". Mackey further explained that Wren considered "a 'perpend ashlar' was one with polished ends, each of which would lie in a surface of the wall; in that case a 'rough ashlar' was not a formless mass of rock, but was a stone ready for use, no surface of which would appear in the building walls; it was unfinished in the sense of unpolished. In other records, of which only a few have been found, a 'perpend' ashlar was of stone cut with a key in it to interlock with a second stone cut correspondingly".

Wren, being an operative Mason, considered a perfect stone to be one that was already prepared for his needs as the builder in the construction of the edifice he was currently constructing. In retrospect, it makes little sense to spend extra time squaring a stone which will not be seen in the middle of a wall. The stone just needed to fit well and can be squared and leveled with the other stones which made up the wall.

While I believe that it is a person's duty to strive for perfection and try to become the best person that they can become, I have come to believe the teachings of Freemasonry are not trying to make each one of us into a brick but, like the speculative use of the common gavel to break off the rough corners, divest you from all vices and superfluities and to makes you into a good citizen who strives to follow the Volume of Sacred Law and to be a humble servant to his fellow man.

Sadly, in my opinion, many of us in our quest for perfection tend to attempt to become the brick; we use man made materials and form ourselves to appear perfect before the world, to hone ourselves not for the use of our celestial Grand Master, but to shine or stand out before the world. In our daily lives it is difficult not to fall into the trap of trying to look perfect before the world. Some of us strive to own the perfect house or car, or make our family appear to be perfect before the world. In these days of social media, the temptation has become even stronger. Even within the bounds of our fraternity this can happen.

Freemasons are obligated to help each other. To become one sacred band of friends and Brothers. I cannot think of any part of our obligations where it calls on us to become better men for the purpose of bettering ourselves or for personal gain. The obligations we take before our brethren in the name of our creator are to help the Brethren of the lodge, and the Craft thereby, their wives, widows and orphans, just as we hope, God forbid, the others would likewise help us during times of despair.

Lofty titles, elaborate regalia and power within our fraternity can lead a Brother astray and cause him to forget the reasons he once kneeled at the altar of Freemasonry. It's easy to fall into this trap.

As the band Pink Floyd observed we don't want to become "just another brick in the wall". A square, soulless, almost Godless instrument of society; one of many, which cannot be distinguished from one another.

The only way our fraternity to continue is for each one of us to remember the reasons why we endeavor to become better men: to make our living stones fit into that spiritual building, using the cement of Brotherly love and affection to help unite and level us, guided by the Great Architect's hands.

Originally published in the *Journal of the Masonic Society* Issue No. 34, Fall 2016

11. Blinded by the light

Blinded by the light. It sounds like the perfect title for a Masonic article, but in this instance the phrase is the title of a song. Please, bear with me. "Blinded by the Light" was a song written and recorded in 1972, by a young Bruce Springsteen. It received more commercial success in 1977, when the song was covered by the sixties group Manfred Mann's Earth Band.

Throughout my childhood I can remember singing along when it would come on the radio. I sang what I thought were the lyrics from the 1970s through the 2000s, never really thinking about the meaning of the words I was singing. I just sang the words I thought that I had heard many decades before.

It wasn't until recently when I was listening to a talk show where the topic was "misunderstood song lyrics" that I discovered I had been singing this song incorrectly for nearly three decades! It didn't ruin my day, but the realization did make me stop and ponder. I could have blamed my misinterpretation of the words on the fuzzy AM radio signal coming through the single speaker in my parent's car, or the pronunciation and diction skills of Manfred Mann, but I decided my folly lay with my lack of curiosity, my willingness to accept what I thought I heard and not bothering to seek out the real meaning of the words I was singing.

When I became an Entered Apprentice, I began to spend every free moment I had memorizing the ritual. I started to learn the catechisms for each degree. Once I was raised, I began to try to memorize every word of the ritual with the goal of delivering my performance without a flaw.

The Brethren of my lodge were elated to have someone willing to learn and began to give me pieces of degree work that they had been performing for years or had been neglecting for many years due to declining numbers. My ability to memorize began to travel. As I joined more Masonic bodies, I was asked to memorize even more ritual. Hour after hour I spent alone, mumbling pieces of ritual to myself. It was difficult trying to juggle the various parts but being a new Mason I thought that being able to spurt out as much of the work as I could, would make me a great Freemason.

One day I was having a conversation with an older Past Master. This brother had seen and done it all Masonically. He was old, crusty and had a sharp tongue but underneath his gruff exterior lay a heart of gold. I loved him.

This brother asked me to recite a part of a certain degree. I rattled the work off, trying to be letter perfect. I wanted to impress my elder with my abilities. Once I finished, he asked me "Can you explain to me the meaning of what you just recited?" Sheepishly I had to admit I couldn't.

He looked dumbfounded and said to me in his gruff voice, "Do you often go around saying things that you have no idea what they mean?" I lowered my head and said I didn't. The old man grunted, "This is what is wrong with Masonry today. Everyone is so busy learning the ritual that they never bother to listen to it!"

At the time I didn't fully understand the meaning behind what he was saying, but as I progressed through Masonry, I began to understand his complaint. In our zeal to become good ritualists, we surrendered the whole point of why we were memorizing the ritual in the first place.

The ritual we are given is meant to be a roadmap in our journey of becoming better men. As we study, our curiosity is supposed to encourage us to think about and investigate the words we encounter and cause us to engage in deep thinking and reflection.

Sadly, in the last half century, our gentle Craft have converted the purpose of self-reflection and self-improvement into numbers, and the speed in which we pass a newly obligated Brother through the degrees into a vacant chair within the lodge room is disturbing. We have become so blinded by the "light" of numbers that we consider the ability to string a group of words together and repeat them on demand to be ritualism. This practice is a disservice to everyone in the Craft: the candidate, the new Mason, our lodges, and the Craft in general.

How many times have you sat through degree work performed by a well-intentioned Brother who fumbles through the words, constantly needing a prompt, or who delivers his piece in a monotone without expression or inflection? Although this Brother tried his best, how does the poor performance reflect on the Craft and what does the candidate think of what he is hearing? I've heard it said many times "It's ok. The candidate doesn't know the ritual!". They are right; he doesn't know the ritual, but the man isn't stupid. He can tell if an acting performance isn't good, and it will come across to the new Brother that the lodge doesn't care about him. He might even reconsider whether joining this group is a good idea.

When the Brother makes it through the degrees, he starts to expect that this is the time that all of the secrets will be unveiled to him. Instead, many times he is placed into a chair and told "just learn the ritual and you will be fine" and is given a part to memorize. At this point, he is thrown into the pool before he is ready to float. Before long he is overloaded and begins to deliver a substandard performance. Eventually he will leave the lodge, due to burnout. Once again, the lodge needs to run a new guy through the lodge to fill that chair. It is an endless circle of disappointment for everyone involved. In my opinion this endless circle of failure can be avoided, and our fraternity will cease to be "blinded by the light".

Masonic education not only will break this circle, but I believe Freemasonry will be strengthened from it. Inspiring our newly obligated brethren to learn the ritual and the meaning behind the words will not only begin him on the path toward the self-improvement but will cause him to think about the words while doing the degree work, causing him to deliver better ritual.

Delivering better ritual will inspire a new Brother, and cause him to continue to attend lodge, which is good for the man and essential to the lodge and Freemasonry as a whole. Self-study should be encouraged, and group study should be offered in every lodge. Mentors shouldn't just help the candidate learn to say the words but help him understand the weight of them.

Light and intelligence always beats darkness and ignorance. My suggestions won't cure all our ills, but in my opinion will be the first upright step in its resurrection. Let's bring our brethren to light, instead of blinding them.

12. We are the Working Tools

During the three degrees of Freemasonry, you are presented with the working tools on the degree in which you are participating. From the gauge to the trowel, you are presented with each one and taught their uses, both operative and speculative. These are the tools you are told to use to better yourself and help create your perfect ashlar.

The tools we are given teach everything from how to wisely use our time, rid ourselves of our vices to love your Brother and work with him without ego. If you apply these teachings, you will become a better man, citizen, father, and husband. But if you have no idea how to apply them these teachings are useless.

These tools are wonderful symbols to help us contemplate the way we live our lives. Our symbolic tools in many ways are like tools an actual workmen would use. Without proper instruction we really can't use them to their fullest potential. The old saying "a workman is only as good as his tools" really holds true. It is much like a man trying to build a house with tools he has never seen before he starts the construction. Proper training ensures you will use these tools in the way in which they were intended to be used and to their fullest potential.

To further illustrate this point if a man wants to use his cordless drill but doesn't charge it before using it the drill won't work. He would be wasting his time and will become frustrated. To make sure his drill will work would be to keep the battery always charged. A Mason's tools are much the same way. If a man who takes the time to go through the degrees of Masonry and becomes a Master Mason and then doesn't attend his lodge is much like the uncharged drill. He will slowly lose his passion for the Craft and in the end the teachings of the fraternity will lose its power.

To be able to fully utilize the tools given him he must charge himself by gathering with his brethren to socialize and participate in the workings of his lodge and immerse himself in Masonic education. Without charging yourself with the energy of your lodge and its members your inner battery will grow dim and will soon lose its charge.

Men are social creatures. Sociologist Charles Cooley called this "the looking glass self". Cooley said "The human mind is social. Beginning as children, humans begin to define themselves within the context of their socializations".

Each person we encounter throughout our lives helps to mold and shape us into who we are and who we want to be. It starts with your parents and follows you through school into adulthood. Every person we interact with influences our lives and our futures. We have a personal responsibility to use our tools so that when we encounter others, we can be a positive influence in their life.

As we look around our fraternity, we encounter other brethren. Many of them, we notice, have the traits and characteristics we wish to emulate. This may be your seated Grand Master, a Past Grand Master, the brother within your lodge or even the old tiler who sits without the door. Each one of them have a lifetime working on themselves and learning through their interactions with other people. Sadly, a Brother who doesn't attend his lodge will lose out of these influences and our teachings will mean nothing to him.

A workman must also maintain and his tools and keep them sharp. If you have a new saw but never use it and instead of putting it away properly leave it outside in the elements, the saw will soon become rusty and when you want to use it the saw will be useless.

So, it is with your symbolic tools. When the Worshipful Master presents to you these tools and you don't take them to heart and begin to use them after some time, they will not be any use to you. Without use they will become dull and rusty and will soon be forgotten. There are many ways in which you can sharpen your skills. Many believe memorizing the ritual is the way this is done.

Memorization is a great way to keep your memory sharp, but without learning the meanings behind the ritual it is equivalent to running a table saw without cutting a piece of wood. The saw blade just spins, and nothing is accomplished. By studying the ritual, as well as memorizing it, you will help take the message into your heart thereby protecting it and keeping it sharp.

A nail gun in the hands of a skilled worker is a beautiful thing. It is an essential tool in building, many great edifices throughout history have been built because of a skilled worker with a hammer. Now nail guns can do the same job faster and with less stress to the body of the worker. It is a wonderful tool but in the hands of an unskilled worker this great tool can be dangerous. Proper use of the tool must be learned before he can use it on a job site. Masonic education is much like the nail gun.

To receive enlightenment from the Craft, education is essential. Today there are many sources where you can seek light. Some sources provide good and wholesome instruction for your labors, but many are less credible. In the past many people have written books, either with good intentions or for mercenary motives which contains inaccurate information. Sadly, many brethren over the years have gotten information from these spurious sources, taking the information to heart, then communicated it to other Brothers. This is done to the point that this false information has become "Masonic fact" within the fraternity. Don't fall for these Masonic "urban legends". Become a student of Freemasonry but please make sure the light you seek is true light.

As each one of us are imperfect ashlars using the working tools provided us to strive for perfection as individuals, we need to gather as friends and Brothers to spread the cement of brotherly love as a group. When we attend lodge and interact with other brethren, we use each other's ashlars to sharpen and hone our symbolic tools. brethren, we are the working tools.

13. On yonder book

Elmer Herendeen was sitting in the passenger seat of his daughter's car. He hated being driven around instead of just jumping in his car and driving himself. He had been driving for more than eighty years and seen no reason why he shouldn't continue. Several near misses and a couple of fender benders convinced his kids that he should no longer drive. He hated relying on someone else to drive him to the places he needed to go but he was thankful he was still living in his own home and not in a nursing home. As his daughter pulled into the lodge's parking lot she told her dad, "Have a good time. Call me on my cell phone when you are ready to go home". She kissed Elmer on the cheek and gripped his hand. "See you in a little while" he said as he got out of the car and walked to the door of the temple.

As he opened the door, he saw a group of men sitting around the tables in the dining room. There were so many new faces! Many of the men in the room he had known for decades but recently the lodge had been getting a lot of new members. Something had made the younger generation discover Masonry. It did his heart good to see young men knocking on the lodge's door. There were so many that the usual team of men teaching the memory work couldn't handle them all, so the Master of the lodge asked Elmer to join the team and help these youngsters advance through the degrees. Elmer was happy to help. For many years he had been on the memory work team until he felt it was time to step aside and let the younger men take up the work. But since his wife died, he had been living alone in his house. It was a lonely life although his kids would visit him, and several members of the lodge would come to check on him and drive him to his doctors' appointments.

As he walked in the door Elmer removed his overcoat and fedora and hung them in the coat closet. The Master of the lodge came and greeted him, "Hi Elmer, I have your candidate over here for you. Elmer, I would like you to meet Zac Morrow. You are going to teach him the EA lecture". Elmer took Zac's hand and led him into the temple's library.

Zac was the newest Entered Apprentice, just nineteen years old and eager to learn. He couldn't wait to advance through the degrees. The two sat down at a beautifully crafted hardwood table and the old man opened his briefcase and removed his cipher book. The book had seen better days, the once beautifully tooled leather had become cracked and worn; the Grand lodge seal embossed in gold on the front cover had lost its luster to the point the gold could barely been seen.

Pages were yellowed and some had torn, scotch tape had been used to hold the torn pages together. You could barely read the printing on the pages under the tape. The book's binding had given way and the pages were loosely contained within the two covers, the duct tape the old man had used to try and fix the binding had stopped working a long time ago.

"Wow!" Zac said, "That book is ancient! You should get a new one! I'm sure the lodge has others you could use". The old man frowned "I'll admit it has seen better days but there is still a lot of life left in it." Zac laughed, "Are you kidding? The pages are just lying in there. It's not a book it's just a folder of old pages!"

"Son. Let me tell you a little story. When I was just a little older than you, I got this book when I was on leave from the army. I was raised as a Master Mason right after I got out of basic training and before I was shipped overseas. The men in this lodge rushed to get me raised in the short time I had at home. As I was leaving to go back to the army, I placed this book in my back pocket and started to learn the symbols that make up the cipher as I rode the train back to camp. I read it religiously on the troop ship that carried all of us to England. I found some waterproof material to wrap it in and carried it in the breast pocket of my uniform as I waded into the water of Omaha beach during the Normandy invasion. I recited parts of the ritual to myself as I waded in those waters, trying to distract me from the bullets zipping by my head and watching men die as I advanced to the beach. I think that is what kept me sane during that awful time. I felt like by reciting it to myself the Grand Architect of the Universe was watching over me.

This book comforted me whilst fighting all the way across Europe, until the day we heard Germany had surrendered. And with tears of joy, I read it on the troop ship all the way home. When the Army recalled me to fight in Korea, the book went with me as we served the country once again. I even had it with me when I got to attend lodge in Japan when I was on leave!

Back home this book helped me learn the ritual when I was going through the chairs into the very East of this lodge, and it allowed me to help other men gain more light in Masonry, just like today as I teach you. This book has been my friend, my companion, my inspiration for over seventy years. It has been in my back pocket through wars, weddings, the births of my children. Good times and bad. Through all my travels. And when I put down my working tools and pass to the celestial lodge above, I have instructed that this old book will be in the pocket of my suit as they lower me into my final resting place, so I can continue to learn at the feet of the Master of the Grand Lodge above.

"You see my Brother, this book and I have a lot in common. At one time we were both new and we have both traveled some. Neither of us are in perfect condition. We both share a lot of wear from all the years of use, but we are still in pretty good shape for everything we have been through. I feel like both of us are in pretty good shape considering the shape we are in."

The young man lowered his head in shame. Zac had tears in his eyes, "I'm sorry Sir, I meant no disrespect. I can see why that little book means so much to you. It's your life between two covers." The old man smiled and placed his hand on the young man's shoulder.

"You are right Son. Masonry has been my life and I learned a lot of it from that little book. And I charge you to do the same thing. The teachings of Masonry will carry you through life's challenges if you apply them and don't worry, I took no offense. That is why you are here to learn to subdue your passions." With that the old man opened the book and said, "let's get your life in Masonry started."

14. The box

One day my telephone rang, and I could see it was my mother calling. Mom didn't call me much; she knew I was busy and didn't bother me. When I answered the call there was quiet on the other end of the line.

"Michael" my mother said, "Your father is gone."

I stopped in my tracks. Everything going on in my life now seemed so unimportant. My father had always been in excellent health. I thought he would live forever. Mom and I talked for a little while and I booked a flight for Florida.

Although Mom was trying to be strong, the arrangements were hard for her. After sixty years of marriage, she couldn't imagine life without him. We chose the casket and arranged for the funeral. "Don't forget the Masonic service", my mother said. "I know he would want a Masonic funeral."

I had forgotten dad was a Mason. He never discussed his lodge much although he went there regularly. When Mom and Dad moved to Florida from Ohio he pretty much quit going and he and mom just enjoyed life.

I had no idea how to contact the Masons. I was from out of town, and I don't even know if any of the Masons here even knew him. I googled "Masonic lodge" and found the telephone number. As the phone rang, I got an answering machine. I left a message and my number and pretty much forgot about it.

Several hours later I got a call from the lodge. The man in charge said he had never heard of my dad. My heart sank because I thought fulfilling my father's wish of a Masonic funeral was down the tubes. "Don't worry" the man said, "If he was a Mason, he will have a funeral." I was shocked.

"Even though you didn't know him?" I asked. "I don't need to know him. If he was a Mason, he was my brother. He will have a service." I couldn't believe what I was hearing! These men didn't know my dad from Adam, and they were going to take time out of their lives to honor my father.

"You will need to find his apron and bring it to the funeral home, the man instructed me.

My mother said she knew where dad's apron was. He had told her many years ago where he kept it and informed her what to do with it when the time came. In the closet among Dad's things, I found a long blue tube. I opened the tube and there was his apron! I never even knew he had one. Sitting next to the tube was a wooden box with funny symbols carved into it. I opened the box and the something sparkled when the light struck the contents. Inside were several gold rings covered with symbols, also coins, buttons, and lapel pins. I didn't know what they were for, and to be honest what to do with them. I put them in my car in the hope that someone would know what to do with them.

I went to the local lodge building to drop off the apron. I was surprised at the beautiful décor inside. I remember going into my dad's lodge building once when I was little, they did look alike.

The head of the lodge (or "the Master" as he called himself) shook my hand and told me how sorry he was about my dad.

"I'm working on the service right now. We will do the best we can at such short notice."

"I'm just glad you were willing to do this for my dad, considering no one here knew him", I told him.

The man smiled, "We are a worldwide Brotherhood. We take care of each other and their families."

I couldn't believe in this day and age that people still did that for each other, especially when they wouldn't receive anything in return.

I thought of the box in the car. "I have something else you can help me with if you would", and went to the car, returning with the box. As the man opened the box he smiled.

"Your father was a very important Mason."

I was a little shocked. I never thought of my dad as an important person outside the family.

"Can you tell me what these things mean?" I asked.

"Well, these rings. One is a ring of a 32 degree Mason, one is a ring of a 33 degree Mason." He continued, "this ring is for an honor called the Order of the Purple Cross. All of these are very important honors to Masons but this one is the most prestigious."

He held up a small gold ring, a lot less ornate than the rest of them.

"This is the ring of a Master Mason - the highest degree a man can achieve."

I stared at the box. There was so much about my father I didn't know. He never mentioned any of this to me. "What should I do with them?" I asked.

"Well," he said, "you could sell them, donate them to your local lodge or give them to another Mason in your family."

The day of dad's Masonic service arrived. The whole day was very emotional, Mom was so distraught she could barely contain herself. She just sat on the couch sobbing.

The audience for the service was small, at the most twenty people were there as Mom and dad didn't know many people in Florida. As I sat in the front row, I heard music begin to play. I had never heard the song before, and it sounded sad but beautiful at the same time. I then heard a chorus begin to sing, the words started out: "Solemn strikes the funeral chime".

I looked up and saw a large group of men wearing dark suits with white aprons and white gloves, walking single file into the room. There were so many, I counted over forty men who walked into the room and surrounded the casket. I couldn't believe there were so man Masons there. The man who called himself the Master began to speak. He performed a beautiful ceremony and then placed dad's apron onto the casket with what looked like a piece of an evergreen bush. Once the ceremony was over, the men left the room in the same manner.

When the ceremony was over the Master came back into the room and hugged my mother. He told mom how sorry he was about my dad's passing and handed her a business card, saying, "If you need anything please call me".

The Master then walked over and shook my hand. I apologized to him that there hadn't been much of an audience. He smiled and said, "It's ok, we would have done it even if no one was there to watch it. The ceremony isn't for the audience, it's for our Brother."

After the funeral I made sure mom was taken care of and I went home back to my everyday life. For some reason I couldn't quit thinking about those men who took time out of their lives to honor a man they didn't even know, even keeping in contact with Mom to make sure she was doing ok.

And now, I am sitting here thinking about all of this in a small room. Not much else to do since I can't see. A voice comes from the darkness – "Touch this, it's a door. Now knock on it three times." I hope my dad is looking down and is proud of me.

15. Help, aid, and assist

Being a Correctional Officer in a prison you must be a jack of all trades. One day you are working in a maximum-security block dealing with the worst inmates in the prison, the next day you might be transporting an inmate to the hospital. Each task is different but there is always one common denominator – there is always the chance of danger.

You never know when it will happen and how bad it will be. You could be working in unit, and everything is quiet. Next thing you know there is a fight on your block, and you must call in a special unit of officers to do a cell extraction. You are fighting with several inmates at the same time, nearly blind because the entire block is filled with gas, or accidentally be shocked with a shock stick. You must always be alert and prepared for anything.

It can also be fun too. Among the staff I work with it is like a brotherhood. We all have each other's backs, and we really care about each other; if there is a problem they run to your aid. It reminds me of the brotherhood I feel at my lodge, where we are a like a big family. When I go to lodge it's like a family reunion.

Many of the brethren from my lodge work with me at the prison. I will never forget when I was going through my degrees, my Sergeant would give us our morning briefing, telling us what we were going to do that day, or alert us to a certain trend or something to watch for during that day's duty.

Then he'd dismiss us, except for me. He would say, "Everyone is dismissed except for Davis" and everyone would file out of the squad room. I think most of them thought I was in trouble. Sarge would look at me and give me a certain part of the memory work from lodge and tell me to work on it during the day. At lunch we would go over what I had already learned and what I was supposed I had learned that day. Thanks to this assistance I learned it all in no time.

The night I was raised will be a night I will always remember. I knew some of the guys from work would be there but since many of us work different hours – and of course there is always overtime – I wasn't sure who would show up. I was taken to the preparation room and made ready for my degree.

While hoodwinked I recognized some of the voices. Once I was given the obligation of a Master Mason, I was asked what I desired most, and I gave my answer. My sight was given to me and as I looked up, I noticed all the brethren giving me my degree were in full dress uniform! I didn't realize it at the time, but the Officers of my State's Department of Corrections had their own degree team. My sergeant had asked the Master of my lodge if they could perform the degree for me and asked him to keep it secret from me as a surprise!

A captain acting as Master performed the ritual and explained to me about the Grand Hailing Sign of Distress, and how every Master Mason was under an obligation to help me if he saw or heard that sign. I thought to myself it was like the code for an officer in distress. All these men being in uniform explaining all of this to me really drove the message home.

I really enjoyed attending lodge but due to work I couldn't attend every meeting, so I went when I wasn't working. I enjoyed the fellowship and learning I received from reading Masonic books. Being a member gave me an inner glow I had never experienced before.

Inmates notice everything. The slightest change they will pick up on it. When I started wearing my Masonic ring, many of them commented on it. It turned out many of the inmates read Masonic books or liked watching about it on the History Channel and were always asking me questions about the fraternity. I answered as many as I could. I told them I was new at it and if I could answer it I would.

One day I was serving as the kitchen officer, I always enjoyed working there. The kitchen is one of the busiest places in the prison and is always a beehive of activity. Our prison serves 1500 meals a day between breakfast, lunch, and dinner. It opens early in the morning so the bakers can begin to bake biscuits or cookies and it closes late at night after all the cleaning is done.

The kitchen is also one of the most dangerous in the facility. The "chow hall" is the place where many fights happen. It isn't unusual to have the Special Response team arrive to put down an insurrection or medics to respond to an inmate who has been stabbed, or worse.

The kitchen also has other challenges the average person wouldn't think about. All tools must be checked out and returned to the tool cage. If any are missing the entire facility can be locked down and searched because so many of these tools can be turned into weapons, like chopping blades, can openers and such can only be used by an inmate if they are under direct supervision of a member of staff.

An officer also must be on constant watch of the food. Many of the inmates will try to smuggle food out of the kitchen to take back to his unit and sell them to the other inmates. Being a kitchen worker can make an inmate quite wealthy by prison standards.

"The trash needs taken out", a member of the kitchen staff told me. As per procedure I got two inmates and ordered them to gather the trash to be taken outside to the dumpster within the walls of the facility.

As the three of us approached the outside door I keyed my radio "132 to central, door 165", and the door clicked open. The inmates started pushing the trash carts outside. As they started throwing trash into the dumpster, I noticed one of the inmates had a bulge in his uniform shirt and what appeared to be a plastic bag underneath. He was a young guy and I'd had problems with him before in the kitchen and back on his unit. He had just gotten out of the Maximum facility for punishment for an assault on another inmate.

When I noticed this, I said, "Symon hit the wall" and pointed to the perimeter wall nearby. As I started to pat him down, I felt the plastic bag and found a huge garbage bag full of sugar. As silly as it sounds sugar is one of the most dangerous things you can find in a correctional facility. It is used to make an alcoholic beverage commonly known as "Hooch"; it is made from several ingredients generally found within the walls and when an inmate drinks it, he can become severely violent, almost like he is on a dangerous narcotic. He becomes a threat to himself or others.

As I pulled the bag off his body he jumped up from the wall and punched me in the face, I began to feel faint and fell to the ground. I could hear sounds around me like fighting, then it all went quiet. Suddenly, I heard a voice yell, "Hey you need to get out here, your officer is down!" I heard a bunch of talk on my radio, the buzz to unlock the door and the sound of running feet, then I passed out.

When I woke up, I was lying in a hospital bed. Several of the brethren of my lodge and several Correctional Officers were standing by my bedside smiling. They explained to me that after Symon hit me, I was stabbed by a homemade knife made from a toothbrush with a razor blade melted into it. I had sustained quite a bit of internal damage and been unconscious for quite a while. The doctor said I was very lucky and with a little time off I would be ok.

The officers explained that when I got hurt, the other inmate Harris attacked Symon, knocked him out and used my handcuffs to restrain him. Harris then got on my radio to get help. When dispatchers got the "officer down" call, they called the cavalry, who flew to my relief and secured the area.

Investigation showed that Symon had run up a lot of debts on his unit and was pressured into stealing sugar or suffer the consequences from the other inmates. Because of the attack Symon had been transferred to another, more secure facility and is now facing another twenty years on his sentence for his assault on an officer. Harris was placed in protective custody so he wouldn't be assaulted for helping me. The Department of Corrections was told of Harris's heroism, and he had his sentence reduced by several years as a reward, so at least some good came out of the whole thing.

After several months the doctor cleared me to go back to work. It was great to be back, I got a warm reception from my fellow officers. Even several inmates told me they were glad I was ok and happy to see me back.

One of the first things I did was I went to the Special Housing Unit (or as we call it "the shoe") to see Harris. I wanted to personally thank him for helping me. I shook his hand (which is against regulations, but I thought just this once it would be ok) and thanked him for saving my life.

"Mister Davis, I saw you needed help and was glad I could help you. I've screwed up a lot in my life" he said. "My parents tried to raise me right, but I wouldn't listen to them. My father was a Mason, he was truly a great man. Dad tried to teach me the way to be a better man, so when I saw Symon stab you, I thought to myself what would my dad have done? I knew he would help his brother Mason, so since he couldn't be here, I thought I would do it for him."

He went on. "I know I can never follow in his footsteps and become a Mason because of what I have done but I thought I could help one of his Brothers."

"Harris" I said, "they say you are first made a Mason in your heart. I believe you have succeeded in finding your inner Mason. Just keep using the tools your dad gave you and you *will* become a better man just like he wanted you to be. I know your dad, my Brother, would be as proud of you right now as I am."

It's amazing how things work out. Harris's father gave his son the working tools to become a better man, but he decided to throw them down. Yet years later, when he realized his father was right, he picked them back up again and began to work on his ashlar. I hope with work his ashlar will become perfect. I never had thought about it, but I guess sometimes you don't need to wear an apron to use Masonry to become a better man.

16. The reports of my death...

There is an old story (which may or not be true) about Brother Samuel Langhorne Clemens who is more commonly known by his pen name of Mark Twain. Clemens was raised to the sublime degree of a Master Mason in Polar Star Lodge 79 in Saint Louis, Missouri in 1861.

In May of 1897, Brother Mark Twain was approached by reporters in London. Twain was abroad on a world speaking tour and a rumor was started in the United States that he had become ill and had sadly passed away. It has been said that the rumor had grown to such proportion that a newspaper published Twain's obituary.

When reporters approached Brother Twain about the rumor and asked the humorist for a quote, he told the assembled group of reporters, "The reports of my death have been greatly exaggerated."

When I first asked a friend of mine for a petition to become a Freemason, I was invited to attend dinner with the brethren of my future Mother Lodge. The members of the lodge were hosting the brethren of our sister lodge in Canada. Each year the two lodges gathered, one year in the United States and the next year in Canada, to spread the cement of Brotherly love.

As I sat down to a wonderful meal of Hoosier style beef and noodles, one of the brethren, an outspoken Past Master, piped up and said "I don't know why you are joining the Masons. The fraternity will be dead in five years anyway."

Of course, his statement shocked me. At that moment of my life, I knew absolutely nothing about the organization. For my entire adult life, I had seen the windowless high-rise building downtown that I was currently eating dinner in and never given a moment of thought to the possibility the organization may have membership problems. I ignored the man's declaration and progressed through the degrees to become a Master Mason.

That dinner I attended has now been thirteen years ago, and our beloved Craft is still at labor many years after my brother's prediction. Recently while reading social media, I have seen many Brothers who, in their frustration with the direction of Masonry, have been making the same declaration: "Masonry is dead!"

As a member who has been fighting with the establishment since my raising, I truly understand the frustration these brothers are laboring under; the slow progress of change (please pardon my use of that dirty word) can be quite frustrating. But I truly believe, as in the case of the reports of Brother Twain's demise, the report of our beloved fraternity's death has been "greatly exaggerated".

The year I became a Mason (2002), many lodges were merging with other lodges, or just surrendering their charters to their Grand Lodges. Buildings were being sold to developers or given to local municipalities. It was a sad time for our gentle Craft. There was one lodge in the Masonic Temple where my lodge met that had to call a Past Master of the lodge to come from his home to sign the book to have the minimum number of members to open a lodge in our jurisdiction. It was looking dim for the members of most lodges.

Since those dark days, many young men have discovered Freemasonry through the writings of Dan Brown. Brown made us look cool and relevant, not just a bunch of old men arguing over fish fries and pancakes.

Even though I still get frustrated myself with the glacier-like slowness that our fraternity moves in, I can say without hesitation that even though the movement is slow, we *are* still moving.

Today, more lodges are including Masonic Education into their meetings, and more Grand Lodges have voted to allow subordinate lodges to open on the Entered Apprentice degree. We have even seen some lodges vote to raise dues to common sense amounts (no elderly brethren on fixed incomes were harmed during this staggeringly significant event). Although we still have a way to go, the fact is that we are making progress.

As long as we have men who are willing to stand their ground and not waiver in their beliefs in this institution, it will never die. This beloved group has, for three hundred years, withstood wars, economic depressions, anti-Masonic movements, and dictators who wished to erase it from the earth. We stood our ground, and we practiced our beliefs. The only way we will see it cease is if we allow it to, through apathy, through hopelessness, and through quitting.

I often wonder what would have happened if all of the Brothers who threw their hands up in frustration, picked up their apron and went home had instead stayed and, with other like-minded brethren, banded together and worked as a group to make Freemasonry what they wanted it to be? I have a feeling that many of the issues these men were having with the Craft would have gone away!

We all must work together, brethren. Instead of giving up, try finding Brothers who feel the same way you do and make a difference! With all of us working together, we will soon see Freemasonry awake from its slumber and rise to become vibrant again. None of us can do this alone. Come and help us show that the reports of Freemasonry's death are greatly exaggerated!

17. From the East to the West

It was a beautiful autumn morning in Central California, 1936. The rays of the sun began to cast light on the fruit trees, which were beginning to bear their bounty.

Robert Hayes went out to his mailbox to fetch the morning paper. Robert loved the mornings, even though his love of the morning rarely showed through his usual grumpiness. This was his time of the day to read and catch up with the events of the world while his wife fixed his breakfast. Robert slowly sat down on his rocking chair stationed on the front porch of his modest home. The quiet morning was disrupted by the sound of a truck making its way down his driveway.

The Model A pickup came to a stop near the front porch where Hayes was sitting. Over the top of his paper, Hayes could see the truck was loaded down with furniture. He could see several sets of eyes peering at him from behind the furniture stacked on every available inch of this old Ford.

"Good morning! I'm sorry to bother you sir, I wonder if you could spare some water, my radiator has run dry." Hayes looked the man up and down. "The well is right over there, help yourself", he said with a grumble.

"Thank ya sir! My name is Chester, my friends call me Chet." Chet took his bucket to the well and pumped it full of water. "I do appreciate your kindness."
The man on porch merely replied with a surly grunt. Chet tried to strike up a friendly conversation. "Beautiful place you have here sir, everything is so green. It's been a long time since we've seen such lush ground and those beautiful fruit trees." Hayes grunted his agreement.

Chester swallowed hard. "I hate to ask you sir, but are you hiring fruit pickers? My family and I are good workers, and we could sure use the money. We ain't asking for a handout. We work for everything we get."

Hayes not bothering to look up from the paper said, "Nope! We got everyone we need. Ain't hiring." Chester's heart began to beat faster. After clearing his throat, the nervousness in his voice made it crack as he began to say, "Are you sure Brother? My family and I are awfully hungry, and we are nearly out of money. We could sure use the work."

The redness in Hayes's face began to show as he, in one motion threw his paper to the floor of the porch and he rose from his chair. "You damn Okies!" Hayes said in an angry tone of voice "You damn Okies ruin your ground, taking every single time of it growing wheat, not caring for the land you own and when the winds come and blows your soil to kingdom come you high tail it out of there!" Hayes tirade continued. "I don't know if you are aware of this mister, but the rest of the country is in a depression too. The local folk here are barely making it and they need jobs too! You give me one good reason why I should turn away one of my neighbors and give their jobs to you and your brood? Then to add insult to injury you have the unmitigated gall to call me your Brother! Mister, I've never laid eyes on you my whole life and you think you can come in here and claim to be my family? The nerve you got!"

Chester lowered his head. There was silence for a second as Chester looked Hayes in the eyes, which were red with anger.
"I'm sorry sir. I didn't mean to insult you."
As Chester's shaking hands began to make a sign, he said in a quiet, nervous voice, "I seen the ring you are wearing. I'm not sure how things are done here in California but back in Oklahoma this here is the way we signal distress. There's some words that go with it too."

Hayes face showed his surprise. "Are you telling me you are a Freemason?"
Chester slowly nodded his head. "Yes sir, I am a Past Master and now former Treasurer of Guymon Lodge 335 in Guymon, Oklahoma. "

Chet continued. "Before the devil winds started, I was an accountant. I had practiced for many years. I kept the books and did the taxes for most of the farmers and the businesses in Texas County. Ten years ago, business was booming and all of us were doing pretty well when the wheat prices were high. We had a strong lodge and luckily, we built up a large charity fund. But when the stock market crashed and the winds came, our world was turned upside down. We tried to take care of each other, and we did pretty well for several years. We made sure everyone had food and folks could keep their houses. We had hoped God would take pity on us and stop the winds but sadly, it wasn't meant to be. Banks began to foreclose on all the farmers, and I lost my house. Eventually everyone's money ran out. We tried to hold out, but we became nearly destitute. I traded our family Sedan for this pickup, and we took what little money we had left to join everyone else here in California."

He lowered his head. "I know eventually things will work out. Myself and my family have faith in the Grand Architect of the Universe. He will deliver us to the promised land. Thank you for the water, sir. As soon as I get this into the radiator we will be on our way." Chester turned around and began to walk back to his truck.

Hayes stood in his place, the redness of his face in anger began to be replaced with the redness of embarrassment. "Hang on. Stop right there Brother."

He lowered his head and began to talk in a hushed tone. "I need to apologize to you. Since the economy crashed, we have had all kinds of hobos, sharpies and other sorts pull in that driveway. Every one of them begged for a handout or money. I keep hearing on the radio all about you Okies coming in here trying to take jobs away from local folks." Hayes continued whilst gazing at his boots. "Being a Mason I should understand about charity more than others. There was one point I found myself in a penniless, destitute situation."

As the old man looked at Chester, a tear began to form in the corners of his eyes. "I'll tell you what. Pull your truck over by the barn and if you like set up camp. If you were just a typical Okie with no skills other than farming, I probably couldn't help you, but I just happen to know the local accountant in town, he is a member of my lodge. He is elderly and has been considering retirement but has been reluctant because there isn't anyone to take his place. If you can prove to him that you know what you are talking about, he might take you on as a partner and maybe eventually you could own the place. I'll also take you to lodge if you can work your way in. You get that truck settled and bring the young 'uns and your wife in the house. I'm sure the missus will be happy to fry y'all up some bacon and eggs. She might even have some biscuits. Come to think of it she has been wanting a housekeeper and a cook. Do you think your wife would want the job?"

Chester who was standing in the driveway in shock, said with a newly created smile on his face "I'm sure she would but I've been married long enough to know better than to say, 'yes' without her permission."

Hayes actually smiled and began to laugh "A man of good judgment, I think you are going to do fine here! Get that truck pulled over and come on inside!"

18. I have met the enemy and he is me

In 1971, cartoonist Walt Kelley used the quote, "We have met the enemy and he is us" in his daily comic strip "Pogo". According to the website "Humor in America", the quote derives from *braggadocio* during the War of 1812, in which commodore Oliver Hazard Perry reported, "We have met the enemy and they are ours".

Through most of my Masonic life I have thought of myself as a progressive Freemason. I was above the "we never did it that way before" mentality. I have championed such radical ideas as opening meetings on the first degree, table lodges, ending the prohibition of alcohol within a Masonic temple, higher dues etc., anything that might make an old Past Master's teeth itch and blood pressure rise.

One Sunday morning, I woke up to several text messages from an unknown number on my cell phone. As I read the texts, I discovered the sender was the Chaplain from my lodge in Texas. He was asking me in my position as the chairman of the lodge technology committee, if I allow others administrator rights to our lodge's smartphone app. In my morning grumpiness I replied, "When directed by the Master", and started my day thinking my reply would finish the conversation.

The following night I received more texts from the same Brother. This time he wanted me to allow him to have administrative rights to the app because he thought the lodge wasn't utilizing the app to "its fullest potential". He proceeded to tell me what, I perceived, I was doing wrong. The ideas the Brother had for the smartphone app were all great ideas and very innovative, but as a Masonic webmaster of nearly two decades I knew these changes wouldn't be utilized by the membership because I'd tried doing so before in the past and no one had utilized it then.

Needless to say, I got angry and threatened to resign my position on the committee. "If this kid thinks he can do this job better, he should have the job!" I told the Secretary and the Master. Both men tried to smooth my ego telling me what a valuable asset I was to the lodge, and he could never replace me. After a few minutes of praise my ego was adequately stroked and my temper was soothed, and I begrudgingly gave the Brother the access he requested. In my mind there was no doubt I would have to fix it all later after he screwed it up.

The next morning as I rose, my mind wandered to my actions of the previous night, and I will admit I was a little ashamed of myself. I had become what I'd made fun of my whole Masonic life – a grumpy Past Master with a massive ego.

Instead of embracing innovation, I had slipped into "we have done it that way before and it didn't work" mentality. I allowed my ego to hoodwink me instead of following the old emulation "He who can best work or best agree". I have met the enemy and he is me.

brethren, this is more of a confession than it is a story. I have no high moral or knowledge in which to impart with this piece. Thanks to this Brother I realized I have a hidden imperfection on my rough ashlar in which I need to work on.

I'm sure each of you reading these words, whether you realize it or not, have an imperfection hidden deep within your ashlar. I truly believe it behooves each of us to look inward for imperfection before we continue our journey to that undiscovered country.

19. Recycling the rubbish of the Temple

As Freemasons, we know all about, and in many cases make fun of the dreaded fundraiser. Fish fries, pancake breakfasts, raffles...yadda, yadda, yadda. They are all a part of lodge life. Sometimes a small profit will be raised but in many cases the cost of putting on the fundraiser can be more than the revenue which is generated (not to mention the difficulties trying to beg members and family members to volunteer to work at the event). Wouldn't it be great to have a fundraiser which doesn't require a huge outlay of capital, or the constant arm twisting of Past Masters to "volunteer"?

No, I'm not trying to convince your lodge to join me in a multi-level marketing scheme selling soap powder or vitamins to your friends. But I think I have stumbled across the perfect fundraiser!

Recently on a Scottish Rite mobile app I read a post created by Illustrious Brother Micah Evans, 33° who is the Secretary General of the Valley of Omaha, Nebraska. Brother Evans explained the local Knights of Andrew was holding a yard sale. This in itself isn't all that impressive, but this was a special kind of yard sale. The Knights were holding a MASONIC YARD SALE!

The brethren within the Valley of Omaha are asked to donate unwanted Masonic items like chapeaus, swords, Masonic watches, rings etc., and the items are offered for sale to the membership. The most recent sale brought in over nine hundred dollars from items that would have continued gathering dust in some dark corner of a Brother's home.

When I read about this program my mind began to wander. During my misbegotten youth I used to be the building manager of a Masonic temple and several times a month I would get a call from a widow or the child of a Mason. They would tell me their father or husband had passed away and they had a whole trunk of "Masonic stuff" the departed member had left behind and they wondered what to do with it.

I've known several times my lodge came upon the same issue. In many cases, a member of the lodge would pick up the items and put them in a closet in a dark corner of the temple where these items would reside until it was decided they needed to go into a dumpster.

So many times, you see a Masonic item listed on eBay which were purchased in an estate sale and then put on offer to the profane world for some crazy opening bid (you know the person believes the piece is priceless because it's Masonic, and all Masons are rich). Wouldn't it be better if these pieces of Masonic history be offered to the membership and help to raise funds for a lodge or another Masonic body?

My thought is that if one Brother (or several) would be willing to gather items donated by members or members' families, sift through the donations, throw away stained or broken items and price the remaining merchandise, then before stated meetings and degree work (or any Masonic event) the items could be placed on a table and offered for sale. Capital outlay is virtually nothing, so if your revenue was only fifty dollars at each meeting and you made the same amount over the course of a year, this small enterprise could bring in five hundred dollars! That is five hundred dollars which in many ways would be like "found money", which could be used in a number of ways.

If this venture is deemed to be a success, you might even consider setting up your stand alongside the information superhighway. If you have a member who is somewhat tech-savvy you could offer your merchandise on a site such as Etsy, or even start an eBay store of your own. The sky is the limit!

I'm not saying your lodge will get rich or save your temple from the auctioneer's hammer but let's face it, neither will a fish fry nor flipping pancakes. In my opinion, this is a great way for your temple or lodge to make some money and help recycle some once treasured Masonic items, which would otherwise end up in a dumpster or cluttering your house.

Originally published on the *Midnight Freemasons* website – June 2017

20. My Masonic ring – a history

There are thousands of designs and variations in Masonic rings. Much like a fingerprint, each ring is as distinct and different from the next as the individual who wears it on his finger. From an inexpensive ring made of a dull material, to a custom ring of 14 karat gold designed by its owner, to an heirloom passed down through a family for generations, a Brother's ring not only tells the world he is a member of the world's oldest fraternity but also tells a little about the man himself. Each ring has its own story and listening to these stories can be quite fascinating. Each one, no matter the cost of the ring to the owner, is priceless, because of its story and what the ring signifies.

My ring is no different. In 2002, after my petition for membership was voted upon and my degree work scheduled, I began to look at Masonic rings. I must have sent away for every Masonic catalog I could find. Sitting alone at night, I would look through each one like a kid at Christmas time. I would look at each ring and dream of how it would look on my hand and finally, after months of debate, I settled upon a design. In my mind, it would be the perfect ring for me to display my pride of being a member of the fraternity.

In October of 2002, I was finally raised to the Sublime degree of a Master Mason. The next morning, I went to a local jeweler, who also happened to be a member of my new lodge and placed the order for my ring. I took the catalog to the jeweler with me so I could show him the exact ring I wanted and there wouldn't be any mistake. It was a large gold ring with a big blue stone. The Brother smiled (I'm not sure if he smiled because of my enthusiasm or because he made a sale) and he assured me it would be perfect when it arrived…in three weeks.

THREE WEEKS! How in the world would I subdue my passions for three weeks until my new beauty arrived? I kicked myself for waiting so long in ordering my ring. I finally convinced myself that waiting to receive my ring after my Master Mason degree was much easier than waiting to wear a ring I'd had in my possession for months before I was entitled to wear it.

After a very long and tortuous twenty-one days, I got a call from my jeweler telling me my ring had arrived and I could finally pick it up. I'm sure it really wasn't like this in real life but when I look back at that moment in time, my memory emulates a scene as if in a movie; I remember looking at my new ring with an angelic heavenly choir singing in the background, and as I moved my fingers the rays of light which appeared from the Grand Lodge above made it sparkle. It had finally arrived.

Like a young girl who had just received an engagement ring, I walked around thinking everyone was looking at my new status symbol. The brethren of my lodge complimented my purchase. One of the Brothers complimented it (I think) by saying "Oh my, it is really…large." Ok, so it was a little showy, but I felt that the purpose of such a piece of jewelry was that the world would know I was a member of the world's greatest fraternity.

After several years of wear, my beautiful, shiny ring began to lose its luster. Wearing it twenty-four hours a day garnered nicks in the gold. The blue stone received several chips in the cuts of the facets and some of the enamel in the middle of the square and compass had fallen out. I had also begun to lose some weight, and my well-fitting ring now was too loose, and I even considered not wearing it for fear it would slip off and become lost. While I'm sure I was the only one to see these flaws, in my mind they were glaring. I decided that once I became Master of my lodge, I would consider replacing this ring with a Past Master's ring.

In the fall of 2006, while I was Senior Warden of my lodge, I attended the Indiana Masonic Home Festival in Franklin, Indiana. It was a beautiful day and I got to visit many friends I was rarely able to see since we all lived so far apart across the State. After a long day, I was sitting down to rest when I heard a familiar voice and a hand upon my shoulder. Standing behind me was my friend and Brother James Barkdull, Grand Master of Masons in Indiana, and Carl Cullman, then the Grand Photographer for the Grand Lodge.

The three of us started talking. It had been a fine day and we all commented on the success of the day's event. Brother Barkdull asked me if I would do him a favor and of course I agreed; Most Worshipful Barkdull was a good friend, and one doesn't say no to a Grand Master.

Brother Barkdull asked me if I had heard of the song "Masonic Ring" by Brother Howie Damron. At that point in my life, I had not heard it yet. Jim told me about it and how they wanted to get photographs of brothers shaking hands to show on the screen while the song played at the next Grand Lodge session. We started shaking hands for the camera, but Brother Cullman suggested we switch rings. Apparently, the swap would make the picture better.

I gave Grand Master Barkdull my ring and I put on his. It was a simple gold ring, average size, and fit me perfectly. Once the photos were taken, we were commenting on how we liked each other's ring more than the ring we wore to the festivities. Jim suggested that we swap rings until he installed me as Worshipful Master in a few months. In my mind it was a great idea, I would wear this ring which I preferred, and once I was Master, I would look into getting my Past Master ring. It was the perfect plan.

Over the next few months, I really hated the idea of giving up that ring. Pardon the pun, but the Grand Master's ring fit me like a glove. It was beautiful, and I didn't need to worry I would lose it because it was too loose and I must admit, it felt good when a couple of brethren I knew who had aspersions to be Grand Master someday were green with envy at the thought of me possessing the Grand Master's ring.

In December, the date arrived in which I was to be seated into the Oriental Chair of my lodge. Grand Master Barkdull had agreed nearly a year before to install me as Master and it was a great honor. The evening went very well, I was the first new Worshipful Master of my lodge in nearly six years. It was a great celebration!

Once I was in my chair in front of the group assembled, Grand Master Barkdull and I told the audience about our little swap. Jim asked me if I wanted my old ring back, or did I want to make our swap permanent. With a smile on my face, I agreed to the permanent swap. I have worn that same ring since then. Several years later, Jim told me he had picked up the ring from a pawn shop in Elkhart Indiana. I never asked him what he paid for it but I'm sure it wasn't a lot.

I never did purchase a Past Master's ring or any other Masonic ring. I will always treasure the ring I have. To me, it also proves that behind every piece of Masonic ring there is a story, and that the sentiment behind the piece makes it more valuable than the precious metals it was made from.

Originally published on the *Midnight Freemasons* website – January 2017

21. Brother against Brother – The Masonic Civil War

Brethren, there is unrest and dissension brewing among us. Brother against brother, peace and harmony being cast aside like yesterday's newspaper. Battle lines have been drawn and most have picked their side and will fight for their side until the bitter end. The shot heard around the Masonic world has been sounded and civil war is at hand!

OK, maybe I'm being a bit dramatic, but honestly when I read about this in Facebook groups or hear brethren discuss this topic you would think the lodge room as we know it will cease to exist (yes, I'm braced and ready for the comments when this piece is published).

Since I became a Freemason, I have heard the constant arguments amongst brethren on many subjects. Most of these arguments are good natured and have been discussed by members for years: how to wear your ring, the pronunciation of certain words, how to hold your rod in lodge etc. Most of these make good conversation while eating dinner, but there is one subject that will bring usually good-natured brothers close to blows: one day classes. Nothing will throw peace and harmony out the window as the mere thought of participating in a one-day class.

Both sides of the argument have plenty of ammunition to use. Each has their point of view, either *Pro* or *Con*.

The Pro side says one-day classes are a great way to bring in new members who under usual circumstances, couldn't or wouldn't become members of the fraternity. These young men work odd hours or don't have the time to devote three evenings to go through the degrees "the usual way". A man can walk into an auditorium in the morning, receive the three degrees of Freemasonry, have lunch, become a thirty second degree Scottish Rite Mason, and finish off the day by donning the red fez of the Shriners and go home with the knowledge he now possesses within his heart the mysteries of Masonry and has started his journey to become a better man, just like he was promised.

The Con side believes that one day classes are just a way for Grand Lodges to rake in new revenue from the dues of these unknowing young men who are blind to the fact that "they're doing it wrong", that their Grand lodge is just trying to bolster their membership numbers. "You might as well put in a drive-thru lane at the temple!" has often been heard in the Tiler's room of many lodges throughout the country. Thus, the term "McMasons" has been created. The Con side believes a young man who wishes to receive further light must visit the lodge in which he petitioned and progress through the Masonic degrees as many of us have done since time immemorial. The Con side also differs from their Pro counterparts in the opinion that the man should advance through these degrees alone. Multiple candidates taking the same degrees should be discouraged, or outright prohibited. There seems to be no common ground between these two warring factions.

Sadly, there are casualties in this conflict: innocents caught in the crossfire of these warring factions. They are the ones that suffer the wounds. I have personally seen brethren enter the lodge room for their first meeting after they were raised to the sublime degree at a one-day class, expecting brotherhood, and eager to take his first upright step in his Masonic career, only to be told at the point of a bony old finger of a Past Master that he "isn't a real Mason". To be called names such as "McMason" or "one-day wonder", making them feel worthless and unworthy, and then to be called names by men he was told were his "brothers" and would have his back, who would teach him to be a better man, seems outrageous. Chances are he isn't going to return, and his opinion of the Craft will be forever changed. There is an even greater chance that he will tell other potential Masons how he was treated, and they won't even bother to knock on the door of your lodge at all. All of this, because the man had the audacity to take his degrees in one day instead of over the course of three evenings. In my opinion treating a brother like that, for any reason, is un-Masonic.

Most of us know that Masonry is a lifelong journey; if this is the case, then why does the way a new Brother is obligated matter? Whether he was on his knees in a small lodge room, or in a large auditorium with the assistance of a mentor, that man repeated the same obligation as you did – that vow to help, aid and assist. I don't remember repeating words such as "unless he was raised in a one-day class" in my obligation. Most of us say Masonry needs new members to survive. If we need this influx of new men, why are we alienating the ones we are getting?

We need to treat all these men on the level and help them take their first upright step on their path in Masonry. These men asked to join our fraternity and went to the trouble of going through our petitioning process. They deserve our respect, and the title of "Brother".

Let's put all of these silly differences behind us. In the end we *are* Brothers and deserve to be treated as such. Let's get back to that noble emulation of "he who can best work or best agree". It's time we turn these swords into trowels and restore peace and harmony to our Gentle Craft.

Originally published on the *Midnight Freemasons* website – August 2016

22. Broken columns

Thomas Wolfe once wrote: "You can't go home again". I have never understood what that quote meant until recently. The other day I found out my mother lodge, Three Rivers No. 733, has ceased to exist. In July of 2016, it merged with another lodge in the building in which we met. Even though I haven't been a member of this lodge for a few years, I am very saddened by this news. I feel like a part of me has died.

The lodge was started in the late 1940s by a group of Freemasons who all worked at the International Harvester truck plant in my hometown of Fort Wayne. The group originally started out as a friendly Masonic club called "The Corinthian Club", and eventually the group decided to form a lodge and requested dispensation from the Grand Lodge of Indiana to do so.

In 1948, they received the dispensation they sought and became Three Rivers Lodge UD, named in honor of the three rivers on which the city of Fort Wayne was established: the Saint Joseph, the Saint Mary's, and the Maumee Rivers, where the original War of 1812 was established.

In 1949, Three Rivers Lodge was presented with their charter by the Grand Master of Masons in the State of Indiana and received by Brother Ward Bailey, their first Worshipful Master, at a special ceremony in the Fort Wayne Masonic Temple.

Three Rivers was never a prosperous lodge. It never had a large membership, but they became well known in northeastern Indiana; every year the lodge would hold a square dance as a fundraiser in the Masonic temple ballroom. For several decades the dance was well attended, and a good time was always had. The lodge also became well known for performing the Masonic play "A Rose Upon the Altar" and would travel all over the tristate area to perform it to Masonic audiences.

Our lodge also discovered that a lodge in London, Ontario, Canada had been established by Masons who were employed by the International Harvester company just like the founders of our lodge. In fraternal friendship, the two lodges began to meet each year, one year in the lodge in Canada, the next year at our temple in Fort Wayne. A dinner was held and one of the lodges would perform degree work to exemplify how degrees were performed in that jurisdiction. This happened for several decades.

For many years the lodge was held together by several well-respected Past Masters. True Masons in every word. These Brothers would guide the brethren with sage advice and years of experience, and never in a pushy way. Every sitting Worshipful Master would seek them out and ask their advice on how to proceed on matters (I know I did).

But sadly, like everything on this earth, time goes by, and the columns of the lodge began to deteriorate and crumble. When I joined in 2002, several of these brethren were still able to attend lodge, and even though many of us younger men had assumed roles performing the ritual, these men were still able to assume a role in a pinch.

My first few years were wonderful, the lodge was always well attended. We would open our lodge, conduct business, and then close. Once closed and all the lodge paraphernalia was put away, we would gather in the bar room of the Mizpah Shrine temple; it was a glorious time! We would sit and talk and laugh whilst eating dinner and enjoying a drink. These old columns of the lodge would regale us with stories about lodge events long past. We would laugh until the small hours of the morning. Begrudgingly, we would begin our journeys home, even though our hearts were still in that little bar room, still spreading the cement of Brotherly love. Again, it was a glorious time, and I still think about these meetings every day with a smile.

In 2003, Three Rivers began to have a rebirth. We received several new members who, in turn, began to introduce their friends to the lodge. In addition to all these friends we began to receive many unsolicited petitions, mostly because our lodge was forward thinking enough to have the only lodge website in the city. If someone expressed an interest in joining, we would mail the person a "Membership Kit" containing several pamphlets produced by the Grand Lodge of Indiana and the Masonic Service Association; included in the kit was a petition they could fill out.

It was an amazing time for our little lodge. Nearly every Monday was dedicated to candidate interviews. The first Tuesday of the month we would vote on these petitions at our monthly stated meeting. If the vote on each individual man was favorable, the next Tuesday night we conducted their Entered Apprentice degree. Since Indiana does not require brethren to do memory work in order to advance to the next degree, they were passed to the degree of Fellow Craft the next week. On the fourth Tuesday of the month, they were raised to the sublime degree of a Master Mason. Sometimes we would conduct degrees for as many as five new brethren at a time. One of the members, who was responsible for the large influx of new membership pushed through the lodge, had the idea to write an official mission statement for the lodge: "To create new Masons".

This continued for several years. Our lodge was opened every Tuesday evening (except during the summer months in which we were dark) through 2007. In 2006, we were amazed to discover our little lodge was one of the fastest growing lodges in the state of Indiana. Three Rivers was one of the top ten lodges for the year. Things on the surface seemed great. Our families would gather for cookouts, birthdays, and when a new baby came into our little family. A good time was had by all.

Slowly things began to change; I noticed only a fraction of the new brethren continued to attend lodge. The only new members who continued to attend were the group of friends who had all joined. These men not only attended but started to fill all the leadership positions within the lodge. The little lodge which was started by employees of the Fort Wayne International Harvester plant began to become a clique, a private club for these new members.

As the old columns began to crumble more, it became apparent that most of these old columns were broken and only one or two were still standing. They were not able to carry the weight of the lodge as they once did. Without the old columns there to carry the weight upon their shoulders, the clique continued to create the lodge into what they wanted it to be; instead of a Masonic Lodge, Three Rivers became just a club to pursue this new groups outside interests.

I demitted from my Mother Lodge in 2010, I honestly doubt if any of the current members even noticed as I lost contact with them after that. A few days ago, I heard the last "old column" laid down his working tools at the age of 87. Much like Solomon's Temple, little is left of this lodge, which had such an impact on my life, to show it had ever existed.

It is amazing to think that in the short span of a decade, a lodge can go from being one of the top ten lodges in the State to ceasing labor and merging with a lodge, which at the same point in history had nearly voted to turn in their charter because of their membership issues.

In my opinion this sad tale proves one thing – membership numbers aren't the issue. We are constantly told that we need to build membership, or our fraternity will fall upon the ash heap of history. To me this story demonstrates that if membership numbers alone made a lodge, Three Rivers No. 733 would still be standing tall, with newly built columns carrying the weight of the lodge. But sadly, this wasn't the case.

In the 1960s, Most Worshipful Brother Dwight L. Smith, a Past Grand Master of Indiana and longtime Grand Lodge Secretary, wrote in his book "Whither are we traveling?":

"In all the land there is weeping and wailing and gnashing of teeth. The Masonic Gimmick Manufacturing Company, Unlimited, is working overtime to devise stunts to 'modernize' Freemasonry, to put it in line with ten thousand other organizations that clamor for the attention of the Tribal American. Among its many products we are urged to try are these:

Abandon the 'free will and accord' rule which has placed our Craft far above the mine run of societies and permit outright solicitation.

Make the service clubs. Get busy on 'projects' galore in the best Babbitt fashion.

Go into the organized do-good business in a big way. Find an area of the human body that has not been exploited. Exploit it. Set a quota, have a kick- off dinner, ring the doorbells.

Subsidize other organizations right and left, and, in the doing, ignore, neglect, and starve the parent body.

Feminize the fraternity. Carry 'togetherness' to even more ridiculous extremes than we have already.

Hire press agents to tell the world, like Little Jack Horner, what great boys we are ('Masonry is not getting its proper share of publicity,' complains one Grand Master). Never mind actions; concentrate on words.

Imitate Hollywood. Stage an extravaganza. Bring in all the groups that ever fancied themselves remotely related to Freemasonry. Form the parade, blow the bugle, beat the drums, and cheapen the fraternity.

Let Freemasonry 'take a position' on public issues of the day. Stand up and be counted (assuming, of course, that the position the Craft takes is in line with our own pet prejudices).

Go all out for materialism. Raise money; spend it. Build temples, institutions.

Subsidize; endow. Whatever can be had by writing a check, get it.

Centralize, centralize, centralize. Pattern Freemasonry after Washington bureaucracy. Let nothing be done modestly by an individual or a Lodge; do everything on state or national level the super-duper way. Make a great to-do about local self-government but accept no local self-responsibility."

For the most part our lodge bought into most of the above. We did everything except for what Dwight Smith suggested the fraternity should do to put its feet on the proper path which was: "Try Freemasonry".

Practicing Freemasonry works every time it's tried. A short business meeting to handle the affairs of the lodge followed by an interesting presentation of Masonic education. Not just reading a page from the internet about George Washington written by someone else, but a real well produced presentation with a question-and-answer period following.

Once lodge is closed, a festive board with good food and drink, complete with toasts. Not just a baloney sandwich on a paper plate with a bag of big box brand potato chips.

Guard the west gate. Make sure all who enter are there for Freemasonry and not mercenary motives and are of good character.

Practice true Masonic charity and not some scheme to get the lodge's name in the papers in hopes of building membership.

Dues that cover the costs of running a lodge, not to quote Smith, "at bargain basement prices" to entice men to join our Order. Make fundraising a thing of the past.

There are many more points I could make but I think you get the idea. I guess what I'm saying is, the fraternity is kind of like the dog that finally caught the car he was chasing. Now that he has caught the car, the dog is puzzled because he hasn't thought about what he would do with it if the day ever came if he caught it.

We advertise, solicit (sometimes beg) for men to join our Order. Once we have his paperwork and the initiation fees, we do some quick rituals and there he is, a Master Mason. What do we do with him then? We sit him on the sidelines and move on to the next candidate. After a while he quits coming because he gets tired of sitting in a chair not being used (or worse yet he is told the ideas were tried in 1949 and they didn't work, so we won't be trying that again) and after a while he quits coming.

If we are going to continue to actively search for new members, we need to find things for them to do. Add them to committees, teach them ritual or better yet ask them what they want to do! An active member is a happy engaged member.

As much as I hate to see my mother lodge as a victim of our shrinking fraternity, I take some solace knowing that our mistakes may help you and your lodge strengthen your lodge's columns.

Originally published on the *Midnight Freemasons* website – July 2017

23. Spreading cement?

The trowel is an instrument made use of by operative masons to spread the cement which unites a building into one common mass, but we, as Free and Accepted Masons, are taught to make use of it for the more noble and glorious purpose of spreading the cement of brotherly love and affection, that cement which unites us into one sacred band or society of brothers, among whom no contention should ever exist, but that noble emulation of who can best work or best agree.

I was recently watching a home improvement show on TV. The host was explaining to his audience that when most people refer to the slurry which hardens and creates a hard, unmoving mass, they call it cement, however they are creating and using concrete or mortar. Cement is just one component in creating concrete; it is a binder which holds all the ingredients of the mass together.

It's no secret our fraternity is now smaller than it was after World War II. Some say the large numbers who joined during the conflict was an anomaly, that the number of men who hold membership in our gentle Craft is supposed to be small. Others believe the decline in membership is a cause for alarm, and the fraternity needs to try to bring the number of members back to the "post war" numbers (or even to surpass them) at all costs.

Freemasonry has been trying to replace these lost members for nearly half of a century, trying everything in their power to entice new members into knocking on the doors of our lodges. Slogans like "2B1ASK1" and "I M Committed Now R U", offering one-day classes, discounts on dues, even premiums like t-shirts or sunshades for your automobile have brought some new men into our fraternity, but for one reason or another they have all left the quarries to seek what they are looking for elsewhere. We keep asking ourselves "why?"

Maybe, much like that concrete we have been calling cement by mistake, we are offering these men something we call Freemasonry, but which doesn't measure up to the expectations we have laid out.

If you ask any builder, a sure way to weaken a building you are making is to substitute the quality ingredients of concrete with inferior ingredients. Sadly, many buildings have been destroyed over the years by using "shoddy" building materials in order to maximize profit or to lower the price of a bid in order to get the work. These inferior materials may stay in place long enough to complete the building, but after a while the entire edifice will begin to crumble and eventually collapse. Usually, sadly, many unsuspecting souls who are occupying the building can lose their lives to the builder's greed or incompetence.

Slowly our fraternity has been replacing the quality ingredients that creates the strong concrete holding it together and has replaced them with inferior materials or left them out of the slurry altogether. From the late nineteenth century, when a few intolerant "temperance" zealots thoroughly removed refreshment while ignoring the virtue of temperance by convincing Grand Lodges to remove all alcoholic beverages from our meetings and temples, we have slowly been replacing the quality ingredients that made a lodge successful, which, in my opinion, has been causing the cracks in our once solid foundation.

We have further weakened our fraternity by replacing dues, which paid the bills of our lodges and paid for the maintenance of our buildings and offering Freemasonry as cheaply as humanly possible; replacing the money by holding fundraisers which no one volunteers for, and which are rarely patronized even by the members. The once fantastic food that lodge members enjoyed on fine china placed on a beautifully pressed linen tablecloth has given away to baloney sandwiches and potato chips on a floppy paper plate washed down with warm iced tea or cold coffee.

At one point in our history, the brethren gathered into a beautifully ornate lodge room. The sat quietly whilst the lodge organist would play a light tune before lodge was opened, and a thoughtful evening of discussion and learning made the men feel spiritually fulfilled. Sadly, today we get badly performed ritual done by a Brother who was asked at the last minute to fill the chair. Once lodge is opened, there is the process of listening to several sets of minutes from previous meetings being read in a monotone by Brother Secretary, whilst the Treasurer gets prepared to tell the lodge how much money they don't have. As an added bonus you get to spend the rest of the evening arguing over the cost of the lodge's bills and then vote to pay them (even though everyone there knows these bills were already paid several weeks ago).

The rest of the evening is begging for volunteers for fundraisers or to fix a piece of the building that has fallen down, and everyone tries to escape as quickly as possible. Last one out of the building please shut off the lights!

The last ingredient which remains, "the cement" has been reduced to young men hearing "back in the sixties we had fun, you should have been here then". When the young man suggests reviving these old traditions or starting new traditions, they are stopped cold. They are told "we couldn't do that" or the ever popular "Grand Lodge won't allow that".

Eventually these young "living stones" fall out of our Masonic edifice because the mortar which binds them there isn't strong enough to hold them in place.

The young men who are looking to join are looking for those quality materials we tell the world we build with. They are looking for education, enlightenment, a sense of Brotherhood and friendship, a reason that they are on this planet. They have been told that "Freemasonry makes good men better". That is what they are looking for.

brethren if we want a strong fraternity which will stand up to the storms and trials of the coming centuries, we must replace the "inferior" building materials with the things which made us the strong fraternity it once was.

24. Sometimes we can't see the message for the meme

A few years ago, while mindlessly scrolling through social media I saw what I thought was a funny meme. In the top panel, it showed the actors playing the couple from a recent blockbuster movie adapted by a book that women bought in droves. The caption which was from a line in the film read: "I have a pleasure room; do you want to see it?" The panel below showed a garage full of muscle cars. Obviously, being a guy, this made me chuckle, so I decided to create one of my own. I took the first panel of the young couple and replaced the garage with a photograph of the most beautiful lodge room Google could provide me. Pleased with myself, I posted my newly minted meme to my author Facebook page and on the *Midnight Freemasons* Instagram account.

Of course, many of the brethren who viewed the meme got the joke and they replied with a "lol" or a laughing emoji. But many of the viewers lost their minds and a long discussion began on how this little meme of a couple and a lodge room was "disgusting" and "inappropriate" and even (wait for it) UNMASONIC!

Honestly, there isn't much that surprises me anymore, but I can say I was taken aback at the reaction of some of the brethren who viewed this photo of a young couple, fully clothed, engaging in nothing scandalous, and a photo of a lodge room. They were basing their opinions on the knowledge that this photo came from a make-believe movie with a script that came from the author of the work of fiction the movie was based on. If they did not know about that movie they would not have thought twice about those people. This got me thinking.

At first, I started thinking about how much symbolism we miss in our daily travels because of our biases and prejudices? Do we not see things that will make us better men or Masons because we refuse to look past the things we think we have learned already? I realize symbolism is subjective and not everyone finds the same meaning from the same symbol, but is this why? Esoteric scholars can answer these questions much better than I can. I am a layman on the subject, so I will let others with much more experience pick up the mantle and take it from here.

I have also wondered how much we all would be different if we were stripped of our preconceived notions and prejudices. I admit I have some, I believe we all do to some extent. These days everyone's minds automatically jump to the topic of race when they hear the word, prejudice. I believe these biases go much deeper than that.

I'm sure you have heard someone give their opinion on a political candidate or an election that may differ from yours, and you may perceive them to be something they aren't from that belief. You may discover someone practices a religion (or does not believe in religion at all) and you might think they are either on the wrong track or they can be harmful to society. They might have the best intentions in the world, but you might think they are a bad person because of your bias. These are just examples, but it could be a bias on any topic, institution origin, or anything someone else does that you don't agree with, or feel is wrong. Do you judge them for it? If so, look in the mirror and remember the quote from Matthew 7 1:3.

7. Judge not, that ye be not judged.

2. For with what judgment ye judge, ye shall be judged: and with what measure ye mete, it shall be measured to you again.

3. And why beholdest thou the mote that is in thy brother's eye, but considerest not the beam that is in thine own eye?

Originally published on the *Midnight Freemasons* website – May 2021

25. The sign said "Alterations"

The sign on the dry cleaner's window, down the street from the house we rented in our new town, said: "We do alterations". We had several articles of clothing which needed to be cleaned and I had several trousers which needed alterations, so we stopped by the cleaners one evening before they closed to drop off our goods.

As the young lady was checking in the laundry items, I mentioned to her I have several pairs of trousers which needed to be altered. "Oh, we don't do alterations", the girl replied. Shocked at her statement I pointed at the window behind me and said, "But your sign says, 'we do alterations'".

She muttered something to the effect that they used to offer the service, but they don't offer it anymore. This led me to feel angry and to certain extent like they were trying to fool me – the phrase "false advertising" flashed through my mind.

Since we couldn't get the service their sign promised, we collected our clothing and decided to go somewhere else. I walked out of the shop angry and let down, and to be honest feeling a bit cheated. What I felt was that the shop lied and had engaged in false advertising. Even now a year later when we drive by the establishment I look and the sign is still in place; I wonder if other people were conned into shopping there by their falsehoods (since there is no place else within an hour's drive that provides this service, I'm sure quite a few).

I'm sure many young men have watched the movies "The Da Vinci Code" or "National Treasure" or read on the web about the cool things Masons do, how our teachings will make a "good man better" and have subsequently left the fraternity feeling the way I did as I exited that shop. You walk into a location expecting to receive the service advertised by the business and walk out disgruntled and confused.

When a young man submits his petition and check for his initiation, he expects to receive training and guidance in ways that will make him a better man, husband, father and maybe even a better citizen to the country in which he lives. Even more so, a more tolerant man who will learn to serve the deity in which he believes. Does a Secretary reading three meetings worth of minutes for thirty minutes make him a better man? About the same chance putting a spatula in his hand and expecting Masonic enlightenment to find him while flipping pancakes will.

Anyone who has ever counted on drawing new and returning customers to their business knows you will never satisfy every customer who walks through your door, but to intentionally or even unintentionally use false advertising to drive new business to your location will in many cases bring the opposite effect. It might cost you traffic.

Everyone has heard of word-of-mouth advertising", which is when each unsatisfied customer will tell his family or friends about his dissatisfaction (or sometimes his satisfaction) with your services and his experience could prejudice several people who might walk through your door. Think about how many times you have chosen, or not chosen a restaurant after looking at a business's Yelp reviews. So, when we as Freemasons state "Making good men better" on all of our recruitment literature, we had better be prepared to offer that service or we will continue to see our new members walk right back out the door whence they came, and they will tell their friends and coworkers, "don't bother joining".

I guess my point is, if one continues to deliver bad service or engages in misleading advertising to a customer base, eventually you will anger most of that customer base and their experience will prejudice others' willingness to give you a try. So, when we tell young men we "Take good men and make them better", and we give them shoddy degree work, baloney sandwiches to eat and lukewarm Kool-Aid to wash it down with before an evening of minutes and arguing over the price of paper towels for the men's room, it might be hard to explain that these things will make you a better man, and these poor men will feel hurt and cheated.

26. Masonic influencers

Recently on a Masonic discussion board I found myself tagged in a post. In the post my name was included with the names of several other fellow *Midnight Freemasons* and other Masonic authors. The Brother tagged us as "Some of the top Masonic Influencers of Today".

This honor put a smile on my face. Not because of the accolades but it reminded me of all those nights, not so long ago, when I was a new Mason reading books and articles written by men who influenced me. Dwight L. Smith, Allen Roberts, Carl Claudy and several other brethren. Men who had passed to the Celestial Lodge long before I ever signed my petition, who had influenced me to lay my Masonic Cornerstone in the manner that made me the man and Mason I am today.

As I advance in my Masonic life, I've had the opportunity to discover other Masonic writers who continue to help me advance in my knowledge, such as James Tresner, Art De Hoyos, and Mike Poll. I am also blessed to be a member of the *Midnight Freemasons*, who continue to influence me to expand on my own writings and to hone my Craft.

While I sat there basking in the glow of my self-reflection, I began to think about all the emails, private messages, and comments on my posts. There have been so many kind words from brethren, who have approached me when attending lodge. Their words gave me the realization that it is those people, who love what we do, that influence me to continue writing. I write for the men and women who keep this fraternity alive every day.

When I think of the men (and women) who influence and motivate me to sit down at my keyboard, they are the folks who spend their morning drive to work, trying to memorize a certain piece of ritual for a degree they have been asked to participate in. These are men who want to do their best, not out of their own pride, but to honor the candidate who will be conducted through that degree. Chances are people will pass by him on his lunch break sitting alone in a quiet corner of his workplace, as he sits eating a sandwich. He appears like he is mumbling to himself to make sure he still remembered what he had learned on his drive to work and will finally commit the piece to memory on his way home. Tomorrow he will begin his drive with a new section as the sun rises in the East to open and govern the day.

I'm also influenced by the Mason's wife who supports her husband's Masonic journey, even if she doesn't understand it all. She says she doesn't mind spending evenings at home alone with the kids as he attends his never-ending meetings. She trusts him even when her man rushes towards the door, in response to a car horn, with only an explanation of "it's lodge stuff" as he kisses her cheek and hurries out.

She probably even laughs to herself as she helps him learn all the "secret stuff" in that book he always seems to have with him. Little of it makes sense to her but she loves to encourage him in something he loves to do. She doesn't even mind helping to cook and clean in the lodge kitchen with the other wives, whilst the men leave dirty dishes on the tables and rush into their lodge room.

Her friends may think she's crazy putting up with all that "Masonic stuff", but deep in her heart she knows everything he is doing is an attempt to be a better husband, father, and man. That's something her friends can't say about their husbands. I want my writings to help him on his journey, for her and their family.

I am influenced by the Brother who answers his telephone at three in the morning, who rises from his bed to help out another Brother. I also find influence from those brethren who help the elderly. Whether it is taking them to a doctor's appointment, or to the grocery store because they can't drive anymore. Maybe even fixing a leaky roof for a man who served the Craft for many years, but due to his advanced age has trouble getting around as well as he used to.

The only payment a Brother receives as a result of their charity work is the satisfaction in seeing the smile on a widow's face as she is told her heating bill has been taken care of. That relief of knowing she won't have to spend another cold winter bundled up as the cold wind blows outside. These men, who understand the true definition of Masonic charity, influence me to keep writing even though there might be a tear in my eye as I type.

It is ultimately about the men and women who make this fraternity work from day to day, despite being tired or weary, and who continue to make this fraternity work, despite the lack of new membership. They do this despite the people who, for their own mercenary motives, say we are going extinct, that we are devil worshippers, or even slander our good name among the profane. They know the truth of what we stand for and will continue to labor in the quarries until that day the Grand Master of the Universe tells them to lay down their working tools and enter into eternal rest.

These men are my biggest influencers. The men that despite everything, grumpy Past Masters, Grand Lodge red tape, trying to serve in multiple offices, or whatever makes them think about walking away from Freemasonry, continues on and doesn't quit. Those are my biggest influencers. As long as they don't quit and continue to be Freemasons, I will continue to write. Thank you, brethren, for all you do.

27. Freemasonry and the Chinese Bamboo Tree

Not long ago I saw a video of a motivational talk given by a man named Les Brown. In this talk, Mr. Brown began to explain how a person's life and their success is like growing a Chinese Bamboo Tree.

The Chinese Bamboo Tree isn't easy to grow, the ground in which the seed is planted must be watered and fertilized every day without fail for five years, but the tree doesn't sprout until the fifth year. After those five years, the grower's patience and hard work are rewarded when the tree grows over ninety feet tall in that fifth year.

Brown explains in the video how many people will allow the tree to die because they get discouraged doing all that work, spending all the time fertilizing the soil and watering the seed without seeing any progress from all their labors. They begin to lose faith in the process or their own abilities, or even worse, they begin to listen to naysayers and the tree dies when they give up the hard work needed to make the tree come alive.

In today's microwave society where we want to start out at the top of the heap and success is assured, many of us will become frustrated when the goal we want to reach or the objective we have in mind doesn't happen right away or fails to fall into place on the first attempt. Many times, we get frustrated or dejected and we begin to listen to that little voice in the back of our head, or worse yet, those who don't want you to succeed because of their own agendas and prejudices. We give up, move on and the Chinese Bamboo Tree seed we planted will wither and die because we quit watering and fertilizing the ground in which it was planted.

Brethren, in my opinion, Masonic renewal is much like that tree. In the decade and a half since I was raised to the sublime degree, I've begun to get interested in the Masonic renewal movement. I have worked with many dedicated Masons who put their lives and treasure into the Craft with the hope of making Freemasonry grow strong again, and to help it take its legitimate place in society. But I also watch them grow weary in their labors and slowly give in to the naysayers who place obstructions in their path. They either don't see the progress being made or the tree of their labors isn't sprouting quickly enough, or even worse, their skin gets too thin when dealing with those who wish the fraternity to stay as it has for the last half-century. Sadly, they just throw their hands up in the air, leave our speculative quarries and give up on Masonry.

It's really sad for so many reasons. First of all, in just the few years I have been a Mason there has been tremendous progress, such as the mutual recognition of Prince Hall Grand Lodges (including in many formerly Confederate states), many jurisdictions have begun allowing business meetings on the first degree, more Masonic education is being introduced into lodge settings. In just the last decade and a half, our progress has been beyond what any of us thought could happen, just a decade ago.

Every year the Masonic renewal movement continues to make progress, it may not be as fast as many of us wish it would happen, but progress is being made, nonetheless. But if we want it to continue to progress, we need to work the soil in which we planted that seed so many years ago.

brethren, the Craft needs you, each one of you, to continue to advance and work toward making Freemasonry strong again. For each Mason who leaves our fraternity is one less man to work in his local lodge, mentor younger brethren and vote in Grand lodge communications. Like it says in the York Rite's Virtual Past Master's degree: "From a grip to a span; from a span to a grip; a two-fold cord is strong, but a three-fold cord is not easily broken." We are all stronger as a group than we are as individuals.

Each one of us has our own strengths and talents given to us by our Creator, whether you are a writer, orator, ritualist, builder, cook...each one of us has a place in this Masonic renaissance. No matter who you are, we need you. Each of you is important and hard to replace.

Brothers if you know a man who is thinking about leaving the fraternity, try to convince them to stay and continue their labors. Explain to them how they make a difference to you, the lodge and to the Craft as a whole. If they have already left, try to convince them to come back and rejoin us in our efforts.

If we want this fraternity to grow strong again, we need each of you, your efforts and support.

28. Often tried, never denied

"I have been often tried, never denied, and willing to be tried again."
When I first heard these words during my Masonic work, I truly had no idea what the line meant. A Brother I know told me at the time that it means no one stopped you from becoming a Mason. At the time I thought to myself that makes sense, (at least as much sense as any of these funny sounding words in the catechism did). But honestly, recently I'm beginning to think this phrase has a different meaning, or at least it has an alternate one.

For the last few months, myself and another Midnight Freemason have been, I feel, targeted by people on social media in order to stop us from publishing Masonic education. Recently, I was banned from a Masonic group and that shocked me. Upon investigation I was told by a moderator of the group I was turned in because, "Masonic education offended them".

Since then, my posts have been reported to Facebook as "spam", and my author page was unpublished by the site because I had been turned in for "offensive content". I wasn't allowed to share posts, or even post on my own page for several weeks. During this time, I truly began to think, that maybe I should just stop writing, sit down in my easy chair, and just educate myself. It was about this time that the aforementioned phrase came to mind. I realized for centuries our brethren have been "often tried" in the public view, just for the offense of being a member of the Freemasons. From the anti-Masonic period in the nineteenth century, when Masons faced discrimination, examples being; getting fired from their jobs, not being able to rent houses and families being forced to leave communities which they had once called home.

During the Spanish Inquisition, men who were suspected of being members of the fraternity were imprisoned and tortured until they would finally, under duress, confess to the horrific offense of being a Freemason. During the Third Reich, many Freemasons were placed in concentration camps and murdered because Hitler was so intimated by our Masonic light, he knew the darkness he preached was no match for it.
Even today there are brethren being tried in the United Kingdom because they are Masons. I have a personal friend who would have been expelled from the college he was attending if it were outed that he was a Mason. Even as I write these words there are places in the Middle East where it is a capital offense to take the obligations we took at the altar of Freemasonry. It seems sometimes "being often tried" is just part of the weight you feel when you wear a Masonic ring

When these accusations were leveled against me, I felt the need to defend myself against them, I knew I was innocent and appealed. Within a few days Facebook reviewed the evidence and found in my favor, my posting privileges were restored, and my author's page was republished. Not only did I feel vindicated, but I knew once the evidence was judged I could claim, "I was never denied".

I am willing to be tried again because I know if I just throw down my working tools and walk away out of frustration, I'm not just failing myself, but I'm failing those who have written to tell me they like my writing and have been touched and inspired by my work. I would also be disappointing all the brethren who came before me and suffered discrimination, hatred or even faced imprisonment, torture, or death just because of those vows we all took. I will not allow a few closed minds and hearts filled with hatred to make me leave the fraternity which I love.

My Brother, I'm sure many of you have been "often tried". Each of us have viewed things within the fraternity that angered or disappointed us. The wagging finger of a Past Master or trying to stay awake during a boring meeting, or something else that frustrated you to the point that you just wanted to walk out the door of that lodge room and never return. But my question is, "Did you quit, or did you decide you were 'willing to be tried again?'" Think about it. Every member who gets frustrated with the Grand Lodge red tape or the ever-present "we've never done it that way", and who walks away, is one less person to help us develop the Craft into the fraternity we want it to be. Each empty seat in that lodge room is one less vote to counterman that crusty stick-in-the-mud who refuses to allow the lodge to try new things. That empty seat is also one less Brother who can help with a lodge committee or serve in an office.

Ultimately each man who picks up his ball and goes home, is one less vote in a lodge, one less-voice for change and prolongs the struggle. Stay, help put the Craft on a solid foundation and make it ready to face new generations.

If we stand up, as a group and declare we are willing to be tried again, there is no way we can, "ever be denied again."

29. With each upright, level step

The Chinese philosopher Lao Tzu once said, "The journey of a thousand miles begins with one step." If you think about it, your Masonic journey to the East began the same way, from the West
with one upright regular step. When I was advancing through my degrees I couldn't wait until I was raised to be a Master Mason. I was so excited to receive my "Masters wages", which I thought would be the right to wear a Masonic ring and have all that insider information and of course, the secrets and such.

As I was going through the degrees, several learned brethren said to me, "Don't forget the Master Mason degree isn't the finish line. It's truly the starting line". I smiled like I believed them and drove myself insane in anticipation. When I was raised as a Master Mason, my feet barely hit the floor and I was running! I wanted to memorize every piece of ritual I could. I started out with a piece which impressed me so much during my Master Mason degree called the "Optional Charge". Many know it better as "On Yonder Book" lecture.

The Brother who performed the piece for me impressed me so much I wanted to learn it, not just of the beauty of the piece but to honor that brother who performed it so beautifully. I continued my run for a long time. I read, I studied, I memorized. I took a lot of offices, and I wore some funny hats. My Masonic journey had become a long-distance marathon. One day a lady in my family who had been a rainbow girl started asking me questions. Simple questions in which an Entered Apprentice should have been able to answer but I became embarrassed because I couldn't answer them. I remember hearing the lecture in which the questions were answered but I couldn't give her any. Luckily the subject was changed, and the conversation moved on, but the embarrassment was still there.

I realized instead of taking upright, regular steps, that I was running, and my journey had become tunnel visioned. I realized I forgot one of the first things I memorized: "To learn to subdue my passions." In pursuit of "trying to improve myself in Masonry", I was off on a journey with no goal, no map and no direction. Instead of advancing to the East, I was just like Moses, walking around in the desert aimlessly. I tried to cram everything in my brain instead of taking a slow journey of upright steps – reading, thinking and conversing with brethren who have been on their journey longer. I now know what the guys at my lodge were talking about all those years ago, that I used my Master Mason degree like a racehorse uses a starting gate; off on a dead run to cover miles and win the prize, I'm not sure they were referring to an actual Masonic Education.

I'm sure many of them, in their minds were referring to titles which I might receive and experiences I would have. But in the end, they were right. brethren, this is just my opinion but after giving the matter some thought, I feel now that the prize I will receive at my journey's end, will be a sprig of acacia and my own white leather apron, because I truly believe the "finish line" is when I take my last level, upright step at the West gate of the Grand Lodge Above where (I hope) I will hear the Tiler tell me – "Well done, good and faithful servant!"

I am now trying to bring focus to my studying. As I am writing this piece, I have just mailed the last lesson in the Scottish Rite's Master Craftsman Program 1: The Symbolic Lodge. I can honestly say, now that I have completed the course, it was a very challenging and thought-provoking experience, and an excellent foundation for my remaining Masonic studies. I hope to start Master Craftsman Program 2 in the fall. I still read as much as I used to but now, I am also trying to think about the words I just read on the printed page. As if I were attempting a lavish banquet but instead of trying to devour every morsel of food there is to offer and make myself sick; to just pick a few of the tastiest treats and savor them. Eating this way is better for your body and I believe studying this way is healthier for your mind.

I hope this will not only help me retain more information but also, maybe help provide more inspiration for my writing. I guess what I am trying to say brethren, is like I was told in the Northeast corner, "at your leisure hours, that you may improve in Masonic knowledge, you are to converse with well-informed brethren, who will be always as ready to give as you will be ready to receive instruction." To improve in Masonic knowledge, or as I am trying to get through my own dented skull – learn and retain it!

So, Brother, just remember: "We are traveling upon the level of time to that undiscovered country from whose bourne no traveler returns." Take those upright, level steps slowly so that you don't miss anything that life is prepared to give you.

30. Counting our Masonic blessings

"May the blessing of Heaven rest upon us, and all regular Masons! May Brotherly love prevail, and every moral and social virtue cement us."

From the first time we step into a Masonic lodge room we are told, "No man should ever enter into any great or important undertaking without first invoking the blessings of the deity." As we progress in Masonry, we begin to encounter the opportunities to ask our Creator for his blessings on our great and good works. But what are these blessings?

Recently whilst working on another essay, I was thinking about the blessings we receive from the Grand Architect of the Universe and began to wonder, "what are we really asking him for?"

I started to think about an old song I would occasionally hear as a child, about counting your blessings. A quick search of Google brought me the words I had long forgotten – written by Brother Irving Berlin, a life member of Munn Lodge No. 190, New York – called "Counting my blessings instead of sheep":

Now I know most of us to pause for a moment occasionally to reflect and give thanks to God for the blessings he's has given us – our families, our home or whatever you personally are grateful for, but how many times have we as Freemasons paused and truly thought about what the Grand Architect has blessed us with as a fraternity?

We as Freemasons are blessed by our Creator to live in a time and in a land that allows us to practice our vocation of speculative Freemasonry in a spirit of Brotherly love and friendship, without fear of imprisonment, torture or death.

The members of the *Midnight Freemasons* constantly receive emails from men who beg us to help them become Freemasons. Some of them live in places where if it were discovered they were even attempting to join our Craft they could lose their Freedom, but despite the threat to themselves and their families they still desire the light we're blessed to receive.

The first time I visited what was to become my mother lodge, I was approached by an elderly Past Master who said "I don't know why you want to join the Masons. The fraternity will be dead in ten years anyway." That was in 2002, sixteen years prior to writing, and I am happy to say the fraternity is still alive, even though the Brother who made that dire prediction didn't live long enough to see that he was wrong.

Through the years I have heard the same prediction that Past Master made many times; and we are still blessed by the Grand Architect of the Universe to still be here and practicing our Craft. Sadly, more recently, I have been reading essays by Brothers that the Masonic skies are falling again.

These Brothers are using statistical data compiled over the last century to show the loss of membership, and if the statistics *are* correct, we are losing members, and the Masonic fraternity will die within a few years.

But brethren, numbers are just that, numbers. They don't take into consideration the spirit of the individual Freemason and his determination. If you have read those recent essays, or if you are reading these words now, it is apparent that you have either have a love of, or at least an interest in Freemasonry; and if there are still men who are Freemasons in their heart, no one will allow the fraternity to pass away.

If you have ever studied the history of Freemasonry, you know that our Craft has survived the inquisition, the anti-Masonic period here in America, the Nazi era in Europe where our brethren were tortured and murdered and put in concentration camps. We've survived the false prophets who've lied about us for centuries, claiming we're guilty of everything from murder to demon worship, as we supposedly attempt world domination. No matter what lies, or discrimination have been thrown at us over three hundred years, we are still standing upright like a stone wall composed of living stones, held together by the cement of Brotherly love which still unites us. Much like a forest fire which decimates a woodland, when the fire is extinguished nature will begin to regrow, and that land which was scorched will grow back lush and stronger than before.

Brethren, I would be a liar if said Freemasonry doesn't have problems, we all know it does. But this piece isn't meant to address them or illustrate them. The message I am trying to convey is, we as a fraternity need to embrace the blessings given by the Grand Architect of the Universe and begin to work together using That Noble Contention, or rather an emulation, of who best can work and best agree, in order to rebuild Freemasonry. And Brethren, negative attitudes and noncooperation will not light our path; we are totally in control of our own destiny. If we want to survive, we must begin to work together.

31. Is your lodge a carrot, egg, or coffee bean?

A few weeks ago, I attended a class and the class leader read a piece entitled "Are You a Carrot, Egg, or Coffee Bean?" The piece was meant for personal reflection, but I began to wonder if this same premise could be used to gauge the condition of a lodge?

The essay is about a young girl who feels her life is hopeless and confides in her mother as to how she feels that she can't go on with life. Her mother takes her to the kitchen and boils three pots of water. In each pot, the mother places carrots, eggs, and ground coffee beans. Once each one has finished boiling the mother places each into a bowl.

She told her daughter to touch the carrots. The daughter noticed that the once hard vegetable was now soft. The mother then told her to reach into the other bowl and begin to peel the egg. The daughter noticed how the once liquid center of the egg, which had been protected by its hard shell, was now hardened. Her mother told her to pick up the third bowl and smell the coffee. The girl smiled when she picked up the bowl and smelled the aroma of the now freshly brewed coffee.

After looking at each bowl, the confused daughter asked her mother what the point of this display was.

Her mother told her daughter, "No one knows how they will react until tested by adversity and difficult situations". She continued, "Some people, like the once hard carrot, will turn soft when troubles come. Others who seem to be fragile will toughen when things get difficult. Some people are like the coffee, when the tough times come, they change the boiling water into something pleasant."

Much like a fingerprint or a snowflake, each Masonic lodge is different. They each have their own personality, history, and traditions. In good times most lodges will thrive and prosper, but when tough times begin to arrive on their doorsteps, you will begin to see how a lodge will react.

A lodge with weak leadership and with no direction will see its membership begin to decline; their building will become derelict and sadly, in some cases, the lodge may survive for a while, but without a change in direction it will become soft like the carrot and cease to exist.

Another lodge may be just as strong as in good times but if something happens to disrupt the harmony of the lodge, or if they experience a crisis, they may react in a totally different way. Unlike the lodge we compared to a carrot in the example above, the members of a lodge may, in a stressful situation throw harmony to the sideline and instead of working together, the members may begin to argue and start blaming each other for the hard times the lodge has to endure.

Many times, the membership – if they don't drop out due to the arguing and finger pointing – will begin to form factions and instead of working together, they will work on their own solution or do their best to destroy the opposing faction's attempts to run the lodge or curb the adversity. After a while the angry words and finger pointing leads to hurt feelings and much like the boiled egg, the membership will begin to harden and not attend meetings, which leads to suspensions of non-payment of dues because their view of the fraternity has hardened. After a while the "egg" lodge, much like that of the soft carrot will cease to exist and will soon become just another footnote in a Grand Lodge proceedings book sitting on a shelf, while their once proud building becomes another empty building the inhabiting city has to decide the fate of.

The third lodge is just like the other two; in good times the brethren meet in peace and harmony, they have a steady stream of new candidates who become engaged and are an integral part of the workings of the lodge. Some men love ritual, so they endeavor to become ritualists and help the lodge with degree work. Others love to cook, so they spend their time preparing nutritious and delicious meals for members and guests who visit their lodge. Other men are good with their hands and gravitate to the building committee to help keep the roof over their brethren's heads.

While each man leads with his strength, they all gather together for such things as Masonic charity, helping their elderly membership, or their lodge widows or helping to provide a joyous Christmas morning to the children of a Brother who just lost his job and needs a little help during hard times. Since each man is happy serving in his own way, there is less arguing about how things are done in the lodge, and they work together for the common good. Since they all work together, the membership of this lodge, like the coffee beans, will be able to convert what one sees as adversity into a challenge, and when the bubbling waters calm, what is left a stronger and more pleasant experience that everyone can enjoy.

Brethren, I am sure each of us who have circled the Masonic altar a few times have seen examples of each of these types of lodges. All of them have the same chance of surviving hard times but it's how they decide to react to the boiling water, which determines their fate.

It's just my opinion but a lodge that embraces Masonic doctrine partially or incompletely, disregards the doctrine in its entirety. They tend to do this in order to recruit new members, which makes these lodges equitable to a house of cards. When will it fail? But if a lodge builds a sound foundation on Masonic teachings, values every member and their talents, then uses those member's talents to their fullest potential (not just sticking him in an officer line and move him up until he is Master or worse yet just quits attending), a lodge can not only weather any storm but much like the coffee beans in boiling water, will become palatable.

32. Plenty, health, and peace

I guess as one gets older, we begin to reflect on life: your future and the place from whence you came. It's almost as if the Grand Architect has removed the hoodwink from your eyes and you begin to see everything that has been laid out for you. You begin to see how the decisions you made in the past has affected where you are, for the good or the bad, or maybe even both.

Not long ago I was in the middle of something and the wages of a Fellowcraft – corn, wine, and oil – which denote "Plenty, Health and Peace" flashed into my mind. I have heard about these wages and the explanation for them hundreds of times while sitting in a lodge watching the degree being performed but I never really thought about them until that moment.

In my older mind these wages suddenly made total sense to me. Much like many things in Masonry the physical wages mentioned were nothing more than symbolism for the "secret" to a happy life.

Plenty: All my life I thought to have a great life a person had to be rich. I never truly believed the old phrase "Money doesn't buy happiness" because I knew from experience poverty sure didn't make me happy. So, I spent much of my youth and adult life trying to pursue wealth, always dreaming of that one day I would have it all and I would finally be happy. A nice car, a big house and lots of cash so I could do anything I wanted. I really thought a person couldn't be happy unless he was extremely wealthy.

Today I am far from rich, and realize I never will be, and honestly, I am OK with that. It took me years to realize it wasn't wealth beyond my wildest dreams I was in pursuit of, it was "plenty"!

I have never been a person who was impressed by named brands in clothing, a flashy car with a status filled logo, or a large mansion with a sauna or room for a pony. So, my fixation on wealth never really made sense but, in my zeal to build a large bank account, I just wanted enough to make sure I had all the things I truly needed. A nice comfortable home that was warm in the winter, cool in the summer and in good repair. I wanted to ensure I could purchase what food my family needed so they could be healthy and well fed, with a nice car which would get to my destination without constantly breaking down or needing costly repairs.

Health: As I keep accumulating more birthdays and what hair I have left begins to gray, I realize how important my health is to me. Much like the old joke that says, "If I knew I would live to be this old I would have taken better care of myself", I have begun to understand what being healthy means to a person.

In my younger years I never knew the definition of "temperance" or "moderation". I ate and drank anything I wanted with no limits. People tried to whisper good council in my ear, but I pushed them away. To this day I truly don't know why I abused my body in such a terrible way; maybe I was trying to fill a void for something missing in my life. Someday I may understand but today all I see is the devastation my actions have left.

Today thanks to the "ghosts of my past" I have several medical issues that result from this period. Don't get me wrong, I could be in worse shape, but these problems have taught me what a blessing good health is and how one should strive to maintain it.

Peace: From the time I was a small boy I lived in a home in which there was little peace and harmony. I grew up a shack in the middle of town with a yard full of broken-down cars and piles of junk scattered around. The house might have been structurally sound but gave the appearance it was always in disrepair and many of the town's residents looked down on my family.

My father was an alcoholic who would drink all evening until he passed out. Until he fell asleep, he would yell and have the house in turmoil, spouting verbal abuse to myself and my siblings, and on occasion he would be physically abusive. We would constantly hear my mother and him argue, usually about his drinking, the condition of the house or other things. The scars of childhood still affect myself and my siblings in many ways. I don't say these things to make excuses but because of the way we were raised I believe we didn't know how to live a normal life or lay a good foundation for adulthood.

Not having a sound foundation to build a life on, I made a lot of mistakes in my personal relationships, and I got in situations that were as toxic as the childhood home I grew up in. Most of my life I searched for the place that would truly make me happy. It wasn't until I found the lady whom I am in a relationship with now, did I truly discover happiness and peace.

I can honestly say I am now happier than I have dreamed I ever would be. Discovering "plenty, health and peace" has led me to a place of calm and positivity; a place I never have imagined I would ever find.

Upon this discovery part of me regretted not finding these things earlier in my life. I started to think about the middle chamber lecture in the Fellow Craft degree which teaches a newly obligated brother that he climbs those winding stairs learning about all the liberal arts and sciences until he reaches the top of the stairs and receives his wages. Maybe, instead of looking at the physical wages and what these symbolic wages denote, we find the true "secrets" of this degree – which is the secret to life and happiness.

About the Author

Bill is the eldest of three children born to Bill and Margaret Hosler, raised in Huntertown, Indiana.

Since his earliest days he had a vivid imagination and a flair for writing. In third grade his mother was called into school by his teacher convinced that he had plagiarized a fictional story that he was asked to write for an assignment. The teacher told his mother, "It's just too good to be written by a child!" It took quite a bit of convincing to get the teacher to believe that Bill had written the story himself.

Bill has had several separate and interesting careers through his adult life, including a decade driving a truck, which allowed him to visit all the forty-eight continental United States and two provinces of Canada. He also worked as a Security, Emergency services officer at a General Motors plant.

For several years Bill also was the building manager for the Fort Wayne, Indiana Masonic Temple. Many of the inspirations for his fictional pieces come from his time as caretaker to the old Masonic edifice.

Today he lives in Bentonville, Arkansas, with his lady Tammi and their yellow Labrador named Happy.

WB Hosler was made a Master Mason in 2002, in Three Rivers Lodge No. 733 in Indiana. He served as Worshipful Master in 2007 and became a member of the internet committee for Indiana's Grand Lodge and is currently a member of Calvin Prather Lodge No. 717 in Indianapolis. He also holds Masonic memberships outside his mother jurisdiction, amongst which is perpetual membership of Ardmore No. 31 in Ardmore, Oklahoma and a lifetime member of Lebanon Lodge No. 837 in Frisco, Texas.

Bill is a member of the Valley of Guthrie Ancient Accepted Scottish Rite in Oklahoma and the Valley of Indianapolis, Indiana. He has also served as the High Priest Fort Wayne Chapter of the York Rite No. 19 and was commander of Fort Wayne Commandery No. 4 of the Knight Templar. During all this he also served as the webmaster and magazine editor for the Mizpah Shrine in Fort Wayne Indiana.

www.uponthesquare.com